KU-769-835

getaway

in Spanish
The all-in-one language and travel guide
Derek Utley
Alison Higgins with Matthew Hancock

BBC Books

Developed by BBC Languages
Series adviser: Derek Utley
Series travel adviser: Matthew Hancock
Edited by Claire Thacker
Audio producer: John Green, tefl tapes
Concept design by Carroll Associates
Typeset and designed by Book Creation Services, London

Cover design by Carroll Associates
Cover photo: Getty Images

© BBC Worldwide Ltd 1998
ISBN 0 563 40051 X

Published by BBC Books, a division of BBC Worldwide Ltd
First published 1998

Printed and bound in Great Britain by Omnia Books Limited, Glasgow
Colour separations by DOT Gradations, Chelmsford

Photographs
All photographs copyright Michelle Chaplow, except the
following:
Robert Harding 1(b), 4(b), 12, 15(t), 17, 23(b)
J.D. Dallet 5(t), 15(b), 16, 26(t), 27
Spanish Tourist Board 13(t), 80, back(m)
ASL/Ontano 13(b)
ASL/Turespana Grande 14(t)
Museo Nacional Centro de Arte Reina Sofia 14(b)
Alfa Omega 18(t), 19, 25(t), 26(b), 28(m,b), 29(b), 92(m,b)
Pictor International – London 20(m)
Martin Mulloy 106

Special thanks to Don Rafael de la Fuente, Director de la
Escuela de Hostalería, Malaga for invaluable help with food
photography. Thanks also to El Corte Inglés.
Every care was taken to ensure that all facts contained in this book
were correct at time of publication.

Insider's guide to Spain | page 1
Introduction
Madrid and Barcelona
The Northern Coastline, the Pyrenees, the East Coast and the
Balearics, Andalucía, the Interior and the Canary Islands
Holidays, festivals and events

Bare necessities | page 30
Essential words and phrases
Numbers, times, days of the week

Getting around | page 38
Travelling around Spain: car hire and public transport

Somewhere to stay | page 48
Finding accommodation: hotels, self-catering, campsites

Buying things | page 58
Food, clothes, stamps

Café life | page 68
Getting drinks and snacks

Eating out | page 76
Ordering a meal

Menu reader | page 84
Understanding Spanish menus

Entertainment and leisure | page 90
Finding out what's on, getting tickets and information

Emergencies | page 99
Doctors, dentists, chemists, car breakdown, theft

Language builder | page 108
The basics of Spanish grammar

Answers | page 112
Key to Language works and Try it out

Dictionary | page 114
Full list of Spanish words with English translations

Sounds Spanish | inside cover
Simple guide to pronouncing Spanish

INTRODUCTION

Get By in Spanish will enable you to pick up the language, travel with confidence and experience the very best the country has to offer. You can use it both *before* a trip, to pick up the basics of the language and to plan your itinerary, and *during* your trip, as a phrasebook and as a source of practical information in all the key travel situations.

Contents

Insider's guide to Spain An introduction to the country, a guide to the main cities and region-by-region highlights for planning itineraries

Bare necessities The absolute essentials of Spanish

Seven main chapters covering key travel situations from *Getting around* to *Entertainment and leisure*. Each chapter has three main sections: *information* to help you understand the local way of doing things; *Phrasemaker*, a phrasebook of key words and phrases; *Language works / Try it out*, simple dialogues and activities to help you remember the language.

Menu reader A key to menus in Spanish

Language builder A simple introduction to Spanish grammar

1000-word dictionary The most important Spanish words you will come across with their English translations.

Sounds Spanish A clear guide to pronouncing the language

How to use the book

Before you go You can use the *Insider's guide* to get a flavour of the country and plan where you want to go. To pick up the language, the *Phrasemaker* sections give you the key words and phrases; the *Language works* dialogues show the language in action, and *Try it out* offers you a chance to practise for yourself.

During your trip The *Insider's guide* offers tips on the best things to see and do in the main cities. The *Phrasemaker* works as a phrasebook with all the key language to help you get what you want. Within each chapter there is also practical 'survival' information to help you get around and understand the country.

Insider's guide to Spain

Spain's historical setting

Spain was colonized by a host of civilizations including the Iberians, Celts, Greeks and Phoenicians before the arrival of the Romans in the second century BC. Various barbarian tribes invaded the north from the third century onwards, weakening the hold of the Romans. The Visigoths, arriving in the fifth century, maintained a certain unity from their capital, Toledo. They were defeated by the Moors in the eighth century, and the Moorish conquest reached its peak two hundred years later with the destruction of the great Christian bastion, Santiago de Compostela. Parts of Spain were ruled by the Moors for almost 800 years from their capital at Córdoba, then the greatest, most civilized city in Europe. Christians, Muslims and Jews in fact lived in relatively peaceful coexistence for centuries.

The Christian reconquest was a long drawn-out campaign starting with the formation of small Christian Kingdoms. The marriage of Ferdinand V of Aragón and Isabella I of Castile in 1479 united the largest and strongest of these and is considered the birth of the Spanish state.

The Inquisition began under the Catholic monarchs, when pogroms against non-Catholics – especially the Jews – intensified; in 1492, 400,000 were forced to leave Spain. Columbus discovered America in the same year, part of a growing global empire which secured a never-ending stream of rich treasures for the Spanish crown.

The Hapsburg period saw the beginning of the demise of Spain at an international level, and the Bourbon succession of Felipe V sparked the Spanish War of Succession against Charles of Austria. Spain was dragged into the Napoleonic wars, the Spanish fleet was defeated at Trafalgar, and the American colonies clamoured for independence, which most of them gained in the first quarter of the 19th century. At a national level, this century was marked by a bitter struggle between reactionary monarchs and liberal reformers.

By the 20th century, growing social discontent saw the formation of unions who formed their own political parties. In 1923, General Primo de Rivera launched a military coup, and his dictatorship lasted until his death in 1930. The Second Republic was declared in 1931, granting safeguards for workers and giving women the vote, but when the Liberal-Social coalition broke in 1933, the climate was ripe for the fascist Falange party to grow in strength. Though the Popular Front, a loose grouping of radicals, socialists and republicans, won the 1936 elections, General Francisco Franco united the opposition, and with a series of military uprisings, plunged the country into a cruel civil war. Franco ruled his one-party fascist state with a rod of iron and all languages except Castilian were suppressed while censorship cut Spain off from the rest of the world. In 1953, Franco accepted a deal with the Americans to establish nuclear bases on Spanish soil in exchange for much-needed foreign aid. The economy began to recover, boosted by the 1960s' tourism boom which brought in foreign ideas. Franco's last years were marked by a new repression as he attempted to stem the liberalism seeping through Spain's borders.

Franco's death in 1975 brought mixed reactions. His successor, King Juan Carlos, appointed a government of Francoists, but political reform led to the formation of a democratically elected parliament by 1978. Despite an attempted coup in 1981, the king sided firmly with the democrats, endearing himself to the Spaniards who still hold him in the greatest respect.

Spain has speedily caught up with the rest of Europe culturally and economically, partly aided by joining the EU in 1986, though recent high unemployment prompted dissenters to call membership into question.

The Spanish people, geography and climate

Spain is the second largest country in the EU after France, and has the most diverse flora and fauna in Europe. The Spanish are a friendly

and open nation who like nothing better than *pasear* (to stroll) and *charlar* (to chat), usually until the small hours. They are generally helpful and courteous to visitors.

The climate varies greatly according to region. The north is green, wet and cold in winter, relatively cool in summer. The high, flat, interior plateau has a harsh continental climate: freezing in winter, dry and fiercely hot in summer. The Mediterranean coast is

mild in winter and hot and sunny in summer, while the Andalusian south has mild winters but unbearably hot summers, especially inland. The mountainous regions are great to visit in late spring, summer and early autumn for walking, or for skiing in winter.

Spring and autumn are the ideal times to visit Spain. June to September constitute the package tourist season, while most Spaniards head coastwards in August, so the main resorts can get busy then, though it is always possible to find off-the-beaten-track hide-aways if you have your own transport. For those into winter getaways, remember the climate of the Canary Islands remains moderate all year.

Currency and changing money

Spain tends to be cheaper than other European countries for eating and drinking out and for some lower categories of accommodation, such as *casas de huéspedes* and *pensiones* (see p49). Most hotels, larger shops and supermarkets accept major credit cards. You can draw cash from cash machines in bigger towns and cities. Change money or traveller's

cheques in banks, hotels or in the special currency exchange bureaux which can be found in the main resorts and cities. Banks open from 8.30 am to 2.30 pm from Monday to Friday, and from 8.00 am to 12.00 noon on Saturday. Some may charge a moderate commission.

The Spanish currency is the peseta. It is written ptas (pesetas).

Visas and entry requirements

You do not need a visa if you are from an EU country or from Iceland, Liechtenstein, Monaco, Switzerland, Andorra or Norway. Citizens from Canada, the USA, Australia and New Zealand are also visa exempt. You are allowed to stay for 90 days before you need to apply for an extension, which can be given at the nearest Police Headquarters, though if you are from an EU country your passport is rarely stamped. Australians and citizens of other countries should check with their Spanish Consulate before travelling. For

addresses of embassies and consulates in Spain, see p101.

Special needs travellers

Facilities for disabled people are still limited. Many public buildings in the major cities have wheelchair ramps, and the Madrid metro has reflector guides for the partially sighted, but public provision is generally restricted. Contact any Spanish Tourist Board or local tourist office for a list of hotels with facilities for the disabled.

Madrid

*M*adrid has been Spain's capital for over 400 years, yet it maintains a lower profile than glamorous Barcelona or the exotic cities of the south such as Seville and Granada. Nevertheless, when you get to know Madrid, you will find that, despite being a modern metropolis of 5 million people, it is perhaps the most 'Spanish' of the country's cities. Its narrow central streets are well stocked with corner shops and traditional bars and cafés to sample its excellent cuisine, or you can escape to the peace of its open parkland and shady squares which are peopled more by courting couples and young children than visiting tourists. Yet there is plenty for a tourist to see within walking distance of its central Puerta del Sol, including some of the world's greatest collections of art. In addition, Madrid's nightlife is perhaps unrivalled anywhere in Europe; few other European cities can be quite so vibrant at 4.00 am, when the summer's intense heat is at its most bearable.

Don't miss

A visit to Madrid's big three art museums:

■ The Prado, the Spanish Royals' and the city's largest collection, which includes works by Goya, El Greco, Bosch and Titian.

■ The Museo Thyssen-Bornemisza, a phenomenal formerly private collection, almost a greatest-hits of painters from medieval times to the current day, including works by Caravaggio, Cézanne, Munch and Edward Hopper.

■ The Centro de Arte Reina Sofia, a collection of modern art including Picasso's *Guernica* and collected works by Dalí and Miró.

A walk in the Retiro, Madrid's largest park; during the week, its cool greenery makes a peaceful retreat, or go at the weekend when it is alive with local families out to see the buskers by the boating lake.

A visit to the Palacio Real, home to the Spanish Royal family and a spectacular collection of opulent rooms; don't miss the throne room and the historical pharmacy.

A wander round Plaza Mayor, a beautiful arcaded and pedestrianized central square, often used for live music or theatre and the centrepiece of some of Madrid's most interesting and historical streets such as Cava S. Miguel and C/Cuchilleros.

A tour of the Convento de las Descalzas Reales, founded by royalty and still used as a highly atmospheric and ornate convent, complete with rooms decorated with Rubens' tapestries.

A trip to El Rastro, a rambling weekend flea market displaying everything from clothes to caged birds and old cutlery as well as many of Madrid's most colourful people.

Plaza Mayor

A look in San Francisco el Grande, a church with one of Europe's largest domes and containing paintings by Goya and Zurbarán.

A lift ride up the Mirador del Faro, a futuristic tower in Moncloa which offers great views over Madrid's skyline and the mountains beyond.

A night out on the town Begin at the atmospheric *tapas* bars around Plaza de Santa Ana and pace yourself for a long night in one of Madrid's many flamenco or dance venues (see below).

Clubs and bars

Café de Chinitas (c/Torija 7), one of Madrid's most established flamenco venues where you can also dine; it is best to book in advance.

Cervecería Alemana (Plaza de Santa Ana 6), a tapas bar with a wood-panelled interior which was a favourite of Hemingway; it overlooks the pretty Plaza de Santa Ana.

Cervecería Alemana

Joy Madrid (c/Arenal 11), near Sol, one of the most popular and best-known of Madrid's discos, frequent-

ed by media stars. At its liveliest after
3.00 am!

Museo Chicote (Gran Vía 12),
another old haunt of Hemingway; a
superb art deco bar which serves
great cocktails.

Palacio de Gaviria (c/Arenal 9), a
former palace with diverse attractions; it combines the chance to relax
in its opulent rooms with areas where
you can enjoy chamber music or
late-night dance music.

La Soleá (Cava Baja 34), a rowdy
venue with some superb improvised
flamenco; tremendously
atmospheric.

Taberna Angel Sierra (c/Gravina
11), a lively bar with vermouth
straight from the barrel, off the
fashionable (and gay area) Plaza
Chueca.

La Venencia (c/Echegaray 7), a
basic but highly characterful old bar
specializing in a fine array of
different sherries.

Torero (c/Cruz 26), a smart
disco/bar playing a mix of chart and
Spanish music. Open 11.00 pm to
6.00 am Tuesday to Saturday.

Have a coffee or
pastry in:

Café Barbieri (Ave Maria 45), an
old-fashioned café on Plaza
Lavapiés, handy for the Rastro or
the Reina Sofia.

Café Central (Plaza del Angel 10),
an attractive traditional café which is
also one of the city's top jazz venues
in the evenings.

Café Commercial (Glorieta de Bilbao
7), one of the most popular spots for a
coffee and
pastry on
marble
table-tops.
**Café del
Espejo**
(Paseo de
Recoletos

31), an upmarket café with an
outdoor terrace and a glass pavilion.

La Menorquina (c/Mayor) The
upstairs salon is the perfect spot to try
its fantastic array of pastries for a
breakfast or tea overlooking life in
the Puerta del Sol.

Café de Oriente (Plaza de Oriente 2),
an elegant place near the Palacio
Real.

Have a meal in:

Carmencita (c/Libertad 16), with
marble table-tops and brass fittings,
which serves up excellent food at
reasonable prices, near Plaza
Chueca.

Casa Labra (c/de Tetuan 12), a
traditional panelled restaurant and
bar where the Spanish socialist party
was founded; great for a meal or
tapas.

Casa Santa Cruz (c/de la Bolsa 12),
once the city's stock exchange and
beautifully decorated, with quality
food and high prices.

El Amparo (Callejón Puigcerdá 8),
considered one of Madrid's top
restaurants, this designer building
needs to be booked ahead and is
expensive.

Lhardy
(Carrera de
San Jerónimo
8), a lovely old
restaurant
which has
been frequent-
ed by royalty,
so expect top quality and prices.

Mesón de la Tortilla (Cava de San
Miguel), one of Madrid's oldest bars
tucked into the cellars of Cava de
San Miguel, the perfect place for a
tortilla and red wine while you are
serenaded by buskers.

Museo del Jamón (Carrera de San
Jerónimo 6) There is a chain of these
'ham museums', the best of which is
just off Sol, where you can have a

Café Barbieri

lunch of *jamón* or cheese croissants under a canopy of swaying hams.
La Sanabresa (Amor de Dios 12), in the Huertas district; very much a local, with a TV in the corner, an endless stream of diners, and very inexpensive but tasty Spanish dishes.
Taberna de Antonio Sánchez (c/Meson de Paredes 13), one of Madrid's oldest *tabernas* with a wooden interior and great *tapas*, handy for the Rastro market.
La Trucha (c/Manuel Fernández y González 3), a small and popular restaurant with reasonably priced and excellent trout and fish dishes.

Children's Madrid

Many of Madrid's squares have children's play areas with swings and climbing frames, while the large expanse of the Retiro is the most central of several leafy parks. On Sundays, look out for the puppet shows by the Puerta de Alcalá gate. Children also enjoy the *teleférico* (cable car) which carries passengers from Parque del Oeste (Paseo del Pintor Rosales) over the river Manzanares to the park of Casa de Campo. This park contains a zoo and a modern aquarium, as well as the Parque de Atracciones, a fairground with plenty of rides for children and a summer open-air swimming pool. Finally, if you should hit bad weather, there is always the Museo de Cera (wax museum) on Paseo de Recoletos.

Madrid's transport

metro platform

The metro
The metro is very well served by a reliable metro system; free maps are available from any station. It runs from 6.00 am to 1.30 am. It is best value to buy a ten-journey ticket, or buy tickets individually from the ticket office or automatic machines.

Useful metro stops
Sol for Plaza Mayor and historic Madrid.
Opera for the Palacio Real and Descalzas Reales.
Atocha for the Reina Sofia, the botanical gardens and the Prado.
Sevilla for the Museo Thyssen-Bornemisza and the Prado.
Banco de España for the Museo Thyssen-Bornemisza.
Colón for the bus to the airport and the wax museum.
La Latina/Tirso de Molina for the Rastro.
Ventas for the bullring.

City buses
City buses are also good; they run from 6.00 am to midnight, with additional less frequent night services. Routes are displayed on bus stops or can be supplied by the tourist office. Like the metro, it is best value to buy a ticket for ten journeys from a *quiosco de prensa* (kiosk) or an *estanco* (tobacconist). Avoid travelling

during the rush hours (roughly
7.30–9.00 am and 7.30–9.00 pm).

Useful bus routes

Number 2: Passes the Palacio Real,
Plaza de España, the Prado and the
Retiro park, terminating five
minutes' walk from Las Ventas
bullring.
Number 27: Passes Atocha station,
the botanical gardens, the Prado, the
Thyssen-Bornemisza museum,
through the elegant shopping area of
Salamanca to Chamartín station.

Daytrips from Madrid

Madrid is the perfect base to see
some historical or interesting towns,
some of which are described in later
chapters.
Avila, with its superb circuit of 11th-
century walls. Don't miss the
Convento de Santa Teresa or the
Cuatro Postes, a shrine just outside
town where the saint avoided being
martyred by the Moors, from where
there are great views over the town.
El Escorial, a huge 16th-century
monastery and palace where King

Felipe II wanted to live as a monk
while controlling his empire. Go on
to El Valle de los Caídos, a powerful
monument to Civil War victims
where Franco is buried.
**Segovia and La Granja or San
Ildefonso** (see p25).
Aranjuez, take *El Tren de la Fresa*, the
steam strawberry train from Madrid
to the verdant Bourbon palaces and
gardens of this town; don't miss the
opulent royal collection in the Casa
del Labrador.
Navacerrada and Los Cotos, two
winter ski resorts in the snow-capped
mountains outside Madrid; in
summer, they make perfect hiking
country.
Chinchón, a pretty village with
wooden-balconied houses clustered
round its main square. Try the
locally-produced aniseed drink,
Chinchón.

Toledo (see p24).
La Pedraza (see p25).

Barcelona

*B*arcelona is the most cosmopolitan city in Spain, with a busy port next to the old town and a thriving commercial centre which spreads inland to the suburbs of Eixample and Gràcia. The developments linked to the 1992 Olympics have transformed the city to the south around Montjuïc, and especially around the port, which now boasts an impressive palm-tree-lined promenade and man-made beach, ideal for an afternoon's sunbathing. Catalan is the official and most widely-spoken language in this fiercely independent region, though people will reply in Castilian if you address them first. Below are the more common Catalan spellings.

Don't miss

Barri Gòtic The medieval heart of the city, with its warren of tiny streets, crammed with gothic architecture, shops and cafés. Visit the 13th-century Gothic cathedral in Plaça la Seu and look out for the main Catalan cathedral of Santa María del Mar, a fantastic domed basilica.

Las Ramblas Five streets joined into one from the Plaça de Catalunya to the harbour which are great for a promenade or a shop. Pop into the bustling Boquería food market, and look out for the Palau de Música, Gaudí's art deco concert hall.

Eixample This commercial district is home to many modernist architectural masterpieces. Head to the Manzana de la Discòrdia and look out for Gaudí's Casa Batlló, which can be found on Passeig de Gràcia.

Sagrada Familia Gaudí's unfinished cathedral, with its eight spiky spires, which was begun in 1883.

Parc Güell Gaudí's garden, north of Gràcia, is not to be missed. Explore the swirling pathways sprinkled with hallucinatory sculptures covered in multi-coloured mosaics, and look out for the weird Hall of Columns.

Parc de la Ciutadella A lovely park which contains a Gaudí fountain and the town zoo, home to the rare albino gorilla.

Museu Picasso A priceless collection held in a medieval palace.

A ride on the cross-harbour cable car, with its spectacular views from Montjuïc across to Barceloneta.

Montjuïc The area on and around this old fortress mountain contains the Museo Nacional de Arte de Cataluña, the city's best art collection. See Poble Espanyol with its replicas of famous buildings from the other regions of Spain; visit the Fundació Miró, with Miró's paintings and lovely gardens. This is also where the Olympic ring and the Palau de Sant Jordi can be found.

A trip up Tibidabo, for breathtaking views out to sea and over to Montserrat and the Pyrenees. Dare a ride on the fairground, perched several hundred metres up the Mount; children love it.

Eat out, have a coffee or a night out in:

La Bodegueta (Rambla Catalunya 98), for delicious *cava* and tasty snacks in the basement.

Los Caracoles (c/Escudellers 14), a rightly famed, spacious and atmospheric restaurant with superb regional dishes.

Café Viena (Rambla Estudis 115), an art deco venue for coffee and pastries.

Boadas (Tallers 1), the oldest and reputedly the best cocktail bar in Barcelona.

Pla de la Garsa, (c/Assaonadors 13), for *tapas* under the wooden beams.

Barceloneta The working port area is the place to pick a seafood restaurant such as Gambrinus, to sample the freshly prepared dishes.

Parc de Mar Wander along the seafront specially constructed to incorporate the Olympic village and have a drink on one of the terrazas.

Gràcia The best *barri* for swinging bars, lively clubs and restaurants. Plaça del Sol is great for a drink day or night.

Tibidabo fairground

Parc Güell

Parc Güell

Transport

Barcelona has a comprehensive transport system with a metro, buses, trains, funicular trains and cable cars which leave no part of the city uncovered. The *Guía del Transport Públic de Barcelona* is free at any tourist office or at the city information office in Plaça de Sant Jaume.

Tickets
It is most economical to buy *tarjetes* (tickets), on sale at metro station ticket offices. These are valid for ten journeys, with specific ones for the metro and buses (T1) or for the metro only (T2). One-day (*T-día*) or one-month tickets (*T-mes*) are also sold.

Buses
Buses and bus stop route maps are colour-coded, red for city-centre buses, yellow for cross-city buses and so on. Buses run from around 5.00 am– 10.30 pm with additional night buses every 30 minutes.
Tourist buses (*Transports Turístics*) run from mid-June to mid-September to take in the city sights. Tickets are valid for a day, and you can hop on and off any buses along the route.

Useful routes
To the airport, by Aerobus from Passeig de Gràcia, Plaça de Catalunya, Plaça Universitat, Gran Via and

Plaça d'Espanya. Also by train from Estació Sants or Plaça de Catalunya.
Trains National and international departures from Estació Sants and Estació de Franca. Plaça de Catalunya for trains from the north coast, the airport, Lleida and the Puigcerdé-Vic line.
Ferries Leave for the Balearic Islands from the Estació Maritim at the end of the Ramblas.
Coaches Estació del Nord is the main terminal for long-distance coaches and provincial buses.
Useful metro stops
Liceu for the Ramblas.
Lesseps for the Parc Güell.
Poble Sec for Montjuïc.
Sant-Estació for the main train station.

Daytrips from Barcelona

Montserrat Take the cable car up the sheer craggy mountainside and visit the monastery which houses the famous Black Virgin icon, said to have been hidden by Saint Peter. Take a walk on the mountainside and explore the woods and scattered hermitages.
Empúries This Costa Brava site contains Greek and Roman ruins dating from 550 BC. Head on down to the sandy beaches and wooded coves at and around L'Escala.
Cadaqués A pretty Costa Brava fishing port with whitewashed houses, which has been popular with the chic since Dalí built his house here.
Figueres Don't miss the Dalí museum, as whacky as the man himself and packed with exhibits.
Girona A delightful medieval town with an ancient Jewish quarter and pastel-painted houses.
Parc Natural de la Zona Volcánica Go crater-hopping in this weird walking country.

The Northern coastline

*T*he north coast of Spain is characterized by a relatively unspoilt green, windswept coastline and a stunning mountainous interior, much of it linked by the scenic FEVE rail link from El Ferrol to Bilbao and Santander along the Cantabrian coast. In Galicia, which the Romans named Finis Terrae, the end of the earth, Celtic fortress villages and funeral chambers dot the landscape. Asturias and Cantabria share a craggy coastline backed by the spectacular Picos de Europa mountains, making these regions ideal for those who like the outdoors, along with Euskadi, the Basque province. Their language, Euskera, is one of the oldest spoken in Europe, while the ETA independence movement has a following in the region.

Navia River Valley, Galicia

Santiago de Compostela One of the Christian world's three Holy Cities (with Rome and Jerusalem) and a memorable ancient town; don't miss a visit to the cathedral's High Altar. Around Galicia, look out for the stone *cruceiros* that point out the Camino de Santiago, a route for faithful pilgrims to the site of the remains of the Apostle Saint James in Santiago's cathedral.

Rías Bajas There are fantastic uncrowded beaches on these coastal inlets, the best and safest for children. Take a trip out to Islas Cíes from Vigo to visit the beautiful wild scenery and sandy beaches of these Atlantic islands.

Rías Altas A dramatically wild coastline battered by the Atlantic, dotted with pine forests and tiny fishing villages.

Hike the two and a half miles to Cabo Finisterra, 'the end of the earth'. See the waves crashing in on the craggy rocks of the Costa da Morte, and go on to Camariñas, an unspoilt fishing village where women continue the tradition of lace-making on their doorsteps.

Viveiro An elegant port with intricate wood and glass-fronted houses, lively bars and tranquil beaches.

Lugo This medieval town is built on a Celtic site with the only complete surviving Roman wall in the world.

Santander A ferry port but also an élite resort with some great nearby beaches and a pulsating nightlife. Take a trip to Santillana del Mar, an acclaimed national monument of stone houses set on cobbled streets.

Puente Viesgo These prehistoric caves are complete with amazing stalactites, stalagmites and cave paintings, best visited from Castillo.

Arenas de Cabrales The main regional town and a good base in the foothills to the north of the Picos de Europa, tucked neatly between green and rocky mountains.

Potes A great base for exploring the south-east and central Picos. Visit Cosgaya on the slopes, Espinama right in the mountains, or go up to Fuente Dé and take the *teleférico* to the top for spectacular views.

Covadonga A scenically located religious shrine where, in 732, the Virgin aided the tiny forces of King Pelayo in defeating the Muslim forces, launching the Reconquista.

The Cares Gorge A must for walkers and wildlife watchers, this kilometre-deep gorge stretches for twelve kilometres, taking you through dramatic scenery.

San Sebastián A chic resort (called Donostia in Basque) set in rolling green countryside with La Concha, a crescent-shaped beach, at its heart. The old town is packed with bars, restaurants and clubs open until the early hours.

Guernika Site of the first mass bombing against civilians in 1937, which inspired Picasso's famous painting of the same name. Look out for the remains of the 2,000-year-old Tree of Guernica where the Basque Parliament has met through the ages.

Mundaka Check out the surfing or take the ferry across to the white and sandy Playa de Laìda.

Logroño This small town is the provincial capital of Rioja with a pretty *casco viejo* (old town), best caught during its wine festival (see p29).

Santo Domingo de la Calzada/ San Millán de la Cogolla Two important towns on the pilgrim's route to Santiago, with monasteries dating from the tenth, eleventh and 16th centuries.

Picasso's Guernika

The Pyrenees

*N*avarra and Aragón stretch out along the mountainous French border with the Pyrenees to the north and the hilly wine country of La Rioja to the south, regions of well-preserved medieval towns and beautiful hiking terrain.

The Roncesvalles Pass The age-old route linking Spain with France through the Pyrenees has been used by warriors and pilgrims alike. Visit the Colegiata monastery with its Gothic cloister at Roncesvalles. Walk the kilometre up to the Puerto de Ibañeta for fantastic views.

Pamplona Wander round the old Jewish quarter of this provincial capital; have a drink in one of the trendy cafés round the Plaza del Castillo and take a look round the Gothic cathedral where Carlos III and his Queen Eleanor are buried (see also Festivals p29). Go on to the town of Olite to explore Carlos III's *Palacio Real*, a fairy-tale medieval castle. Look round Ujué, a medieval fortress town perched on the top of a hill with spectacular views over the south of Navarra.

Pamplona bull runs

Estella This was Europe's second largest market town during the 13th century, still with atmospheric Jewish, Frankish and Navarrese quarters.

Parque Nacional de Ordesa Explore the wild peaks and impressive glacial valleys in one of the highest tracts of the Pyrenees. Follow the yawning Ordesa Gorge or explore the less touristy Añisclo or Escuaín canyons.

Valle de Hecho and Valle de Ansó Popular trekking country runs along these Pyrenean valleys; look out for the ancient, whitewashed village of Hecho.

Aínsa Climb the bell-tower of the Romanesque church for the best views over this picturesque village and the distant snow-capped ranges.

Daroca An amazing walled city founded by Muslims. Try the local wine, then try to count the 114 towers rising from the walls.

El Maestrazgo Get away from it all in this mountainous region of forgotten villages almost untouched by tourism; aim for the heady Puerto de Villaroya pass.

Albarracín A beautifully preserved medieval town – once an important Islamic city – perched above the river Guadaliviar.

The east coast and the Balearics

*T*he east coast stretches from Catalonia (Cataluña) to the flat, cultivated plains and sandy beaches of Valencia down to parched Murcia, drip-fed by the irrigation schemes that replenish its vineyards. Here tourism is relatively undeveloped and you can find unspoilt coastal spots and historic inland villages. Offshore lie the Islas Baleares, the Balearic Islands, ideal for beach lovers and those into nature alike. Their history of invasions by scores of peoples has resulted in a distinct culture on the four main islands which are within reach of eleven uninhabited islands, ideal for picnics and quieter beaches.

Valencia Though a modern and industrialized city, there are lush parks to rest in after a wander around the old medieval quarter.
■ Climb the cathedral for great views over the city.
■ See the *Lonja de la Seda*, the operating Gothic silk exchange opposite the bustling main market.
■ Listen to *Bacalao*, the throbbing techno that fills the central and coastal road clubs, making Valencia one of Spain's liveliest nightspots.

La Albufera A huge freshwater lagoon for irrigating the surrounding rice paddies, a great place for birdwatching. Go on to sample the village cuisine – especially paella – of El Palmar, El Perelló and Perellonet.

Altea This attractive little village of white-washed houses sits high on a hill near the coast, a surprising contrast to the teeming tourism of Benidorm nearby.

Elche palm forest

Elche Visit Europe's only palm
forest.
El Golfo de Mazarrón There are
good beaches at Mazarrón – which
you may share with wild tortoises –
and around Aguilas, undeveloped
and wild but for the odd beach bar.

Parque Natural Sierra España This
is wonderful walking terrain through
the rocky, pine-forested mountains.
Moratalla A castle-topped fortress
town with wonderful views.

Balearic Islands

Mallorca
Though areas get saturated by
package-tour tourism in the summer
months, it is easy to leave the choked
areas around Palma.
■ Take a trek from Andratx through
the village of S'Arraco and on to the
attractive harbour of Sant Telm.
■ Head northwest to Banyalbufar, a
small village perched on a cliff with a
tiny beach below.
■ Enjoy the experience of the scenic
train from Palma to Sóller, then get
the tram down to the picturesque
Port de Sóller.
■ Make the most of the walking
terrain in the Sierra de Tramuntana
near Sóller; get a walking route from
local bookshops and tourist offices.
■ Visit or stay a night in the
beautifully situated Monastery of
Lluc, by the Gaudí Stations of the
Cross.
■ Visit the subterranean wonders of
the Drach caves.
■ Long stretches of white sand are to
be enjoyed in Alcudia in the north of
the island.

Ibiza

The place to go if you want to combine beaches with a vibrant nightlife. There is some stunning inland scenery around the north coast to be enjoyed if you have your own transport.

■ Visit the less-frequented beaches at Ses Salines and Es Cavellet.
■ See and be seen in Ibiza Town where life is one long, outrageous, 24-hour party.
■ Stay in Santa Eulalia for a quieter old town with a lofty Roman aqueduct.

Formentera

A relatively barren island, this is the smallest and least populated of the main group and a makes a good day-trip from Ibiza. You can't miss its long, white sandy beaches: to find the best, head for those round Es Pujols and Platja de Llevant.

Menorca

This largely agricultural and picturesque island offers the remains of prehistoric settlements as well as some thriving tourist resorts.
■ Discover the hidden beaches at Platja Son Saura and Cala Turqueta in the west.

■ Visit Ciutadella, an ancient fortified town towering above a fine harbour.
■ Stay in Fornells, a harbour with two fortresses by a sandy beach. Don't miss its mouth-watering seafood restaurants.
■ Climb Monte Toro, the island's highest hill, for breathtaking views.

Ciutadella, Menorca

Andalucía

This region stretches from the desert-like lands round Almería across the developed coastal resorts of Málaga and Torremolinos to the wilder Atlantic coast by the Portuguese border. As well as Sevilla, there are countless attractions for the visitor, including stunning Moorish architecture, whitewashed mountain villages, trekking and a diverse range of beach resorts.

Zahara de los Atunes, Cadiz

Mojácar A dazzling white town that was popular with artists in the sixties and is now frequented by the hip and fashionable.

San José This appealing resort has a tiny harbour packed with boats and small yachts. Walk a few kilometres west through tall cacti to its long, sandy beach.

El Cabo de Gata Plenty of bars and cafés fill this town near a sandy beach. Spot the flamingos and other wildlife at the nearby Laguna de la Rosa.

Mini Hollywood Have a bourbon in the saloon of the set for the western *A Fistful of Dollars*, always popular with children.

Guadix An extra-ordinary Moorish town where thousands of people still live in cave houses built into the rock.

Granada The Alhambra, the palace-fortress built by the Nasrid Sultans as a living paradise in which to sample every earthly pleasure, is one of the greatest sites in Spain. In town, wander down the labyrinth of tiny streets in the Moorish quarter where there are tempting *tapas* bars at every turn. Climb through the old gypsy quarter, El Albaicín, for the best views of the Alhambra.

the Alhambra, Granada

Nerja A lively, attractive seaside resort with sandy, cliff-backed beaches. Don't miss a trip to the Cuevas de Nerja caves, or to the picture-postcard Moorish village of Frigiliana.

Las Alpujarras These mountains are perhaps best visited from the spa town of Lanjarón for some great walks into the Sierra Nevada national park. This often snow-capped range is packed with unique varieties of flowers, birds and wild animals.

Los Pueblos Blancos These little whitewashed towns cling precariously to the hillsides on rocky outcrops.

■ Ronda is one of the largest and most attractive.

■ Go on to Gaucín with its spectacular views.

■ Visit Setenil where the houses are built into rock overhangs.

Los Pueblos Serranos Another set of lovely mountain villages.

■ Grazalema is set near the highest pass in Andalucía.

■ Stay in Zahara de la Sierra, a lovely red-roof-tiled town perched on a rocky outcrop.

■ Go on to Arcos de la Frontera towering above the River Guadalete.

Jerez The home of sherry manufacturing with lots of interesting factories to visit and sherries to sample.

Tarifa A historic town with Moorish walls and a castle, best known for its expansive beach, a breezy spot which is ideal for windsurfing.

Los Caños de Meca For those into smaller resorts, this makes a good destination, with a fine Atlantic beach; or try the beach by the nearby fishing village of Zahara de los Atunes.

Cádiz Soak up the atmosphere of this ancient port. Wander around the tiny alleyways and pretty squares dotted with bars and cafés, and don't miss the fried fish specialities.

Chipiona A spa town with a stretch of soft sand beyond an atmospheric Atlantic lighthouse.

La Sierra Morena Follow the mule tracks around Almonaster in this exhilarating mountain range.

Córdoba Visit the incredible Moorish Mezquita. Peep through doorways into the stunning flowery patios dotted around the city. Head out to the sumptuous 10th-century Moorish Palace of Medina Azahara, built by Caliph Abd ar-Rahman III for the favourite in his harem.

Osuna, Úbeda and Baeza These quiet Renaissance towns once formed the Christian-Moorish frontier and contain beautiful palaces and churches.

Seville With its winding streets, sunny orange tree-lined squares and breathtaking Moorish architecture, Seville is one of Spain's most evocative cities. Founded by the Romans, most of the surviving city dates from the Middle Ages, when the narrow labyrinthine alleyways were constructed to protect the *Sevillanos* from the scorching summer heat.

Don't miss

The cathedral, which allegedly houses Christopher Columbus' tomb. Look out for the Patio de los Naranjos (orange tree patio), once the entrance to the demolished Almohad Mosque. The towering La Giralda, the mosque's minaret, survives. Climb it for stunning views over the city.

The Alcázar, the Moorish eighth-century fortress-palace. Look out for the arched Patio de las Doncellas with its ornate ceilings, colourful *azulejos* (tiles) and central fountain. The impressive golden dome in the Salón de los Embajadores is where Ferdinand and Isabella received Columbus on his return from the Americas.

The Casa de Pilatos (House of Pilate) is said to be the most sumptuous private residence in Seville. Its gardens and *azulejos* (tiles), though more modest than those of the Alcázar, should not be missed.

The Barrio de Santa Cruz Wander around the whitewashed Jewish quarter with its hidden patios and leafy squares. Cool off in the small cafés and bars serving *tapas* and *jerez*.

The River Guadalquivir Meander along the river, in the unique and brilliant light reflecting from the water.

The Torre del Oro This twelve-sided tower was once covered in gold tiles, part of a thirteenth-century defensive wall built to protect the port.

Barrio de Triana An area of whitewashed houses on the west bank of the river. Along with the nearby Barrio de los Remedios, this is a great area for good and reasonable food and lively night-time bar-hopping.

Head for the lush gardens and parks that characterize the city: try the Alcázar with its Arab, Renaissance and modern gardens packed with exotic flowers and maze (*laberinto*). Visit Plaza de España, with its fountains and colourful tiles; go on to the adjoining leafy Parque de María Luisa.

Take a boat trip to Coto Doñana, Spain's largest bird reserve and most important wetland area, a great day out.

Visit the flamenco clubs to hear the sevillana; try La Carbonería for a venue not too geared to tourists.

Santa Cruz

The interior

*A*way from the coast are some of Spain's most alluring sites, authentic villages and fascinating landscapes largely untouched by tourism. The wild natural beauty of Extremadura, which stretches to the border with Portugal, is relatively unknown

La Mancha

and undeveloped, while the flat plain of La Mancha – with its windmills, saffron fields and the vineyards that produce the local Valdepeñas and Manzanares wines – was immortalized in Cervantes' Don Quixote. Castile-Leon is the land of fairytale castles set up high on the high meseta (plateau), known for its fierce summers and bitter winters.

La Ciudad Encantada The ideal spot for those into interesting walks, a natural park full of limestone outcrops eroded into weird shapes.
Cuenca A unique town perched on top of a cliff which plunges down on three sides to the trickling *ríos* (rivers) below. Have a drink on a *terraza* overlooking the gorge, with the town's hanging houses teetering picturesquely around you. At night, go to the bars built in caves dug out of the side of the rock.
Belmonte An alluring but tiny walled village with a 14th-century castle.
Toledo Its feast of Roman, Mudéjar, Moorish and Jewish architecture, jumbled together in winding streets, completely encircled by fortified walls. Have a drink on the *terraza* of the Parador; the view of the city from afar is unmatchable.

A tour of the Manchegan villages:
■ Consuegra, the resting place of El Cid's only son, with a row of windmills and a fine ruined castle.

■ Go on to the whitewashed Almagro with a balconied Plaza Mayor and a 16th-century open-air theatre, the Corral de Comedias.
■ Stop off in Campo de Criptana, a perfect Manchegan village complete with windmills.
■ Visit Sancho, whose 16th-century windmill still has working machinery.
■ End up in Tembleque with one of the most typical main squares in Spain.
Cáceres Have a drink in one of the lively bars at the heart of the old walled city which was built with treasures brought from the Americas. One of the area's most memorable towns.
Sierra de Gredos These mountains are best visited from El Hornillo, the start of the exhilarating Circo de Gredos walk.
Parque Natural de Monfragüe Special colour-guided paths will steer you along the best routes for birdwatching. Look out for vultures and eagles.
Guadalupe A tiny town in the Sierra de Guadarrama where pilgrims flock to the monastery commemorating a vision of the Virgin. It is also where Ferdinand and Isabella signed their contract with Christopher Columbus. Its cobbled streets and fine central square are little changed from this time.
Mérida An intriguing Roman city packed with archaeological treasures. Catch one of the plays performed in the Roman theatre during its summer festival.
Los Pueblos Blancos Visit the tranquil whitewashed towns of Zafra, Llerena, Jerez de los Caballeros and

Cáceres

Olivenza, each with its own special charms.

Salamanca Wander around the 13th-century university, have a drink in the arcaded Plaza Mayor and explore the Gothic and Romanesque cathedrals of this lively town.

El Burgo de Osma Wander the arcaded streets and squares of this attractive Baroque town; don't miss its historic cathedral.

Take a tour of the fortified castle towns

■ Visit Tordesillas, with its medieval bridge and the Moorish-inspired Real Monasterio de Santa Clara.

■ Go on to Medina del Campo, with a moated castle mounted on a rocky crag and a characterful old square.

■ Visit Coca, with one of the prettiest castles in Spain, and go on to Peñafiel for its narrow castle and wooden buildings.

■ Segovia: explore the spiral staircases, soaring turrets and battlements of the castle. Look at the Roman aqueduct towering above the town, then head out to San Ildefonso de La Granja and picnic in the grounds of what is considered the Versailles of Spain.

■ Avila (See p8).

La Alberca A hotch-potch of interesting little houses adorn this picturesque village, declared a national monument.

Pedraza A 16th-century village wholly constructed from stone. Sample the strong local wine in a bar on the corner of the arcaded square, where you help yourself from taps running along the walls.

La Alberca

Canary Islands

*T*he Canaries are a
group of islands
lying off the coast of Africa, providing a moderate year-round
climate. Though ideal for a beach holiday, they also offer spectacular
volcanic landscapes and lush vegetation, ideal for touring or walking.

Gran Canaria

Gran Canaria

This is a popular and varied island, with high forested mountains in the interior and a desert landscape in the south.

■ Look round Las Palmas, a cosmo-politan city with a fine beach, good shopping and a vibrant nightlife. Don't miss the mummies in the Canarian Museum or a look round the old quarter, Vegueta, where Columbus' house still stands.
■ Visit Maspalomas, with a beach backed by extraordinary desert-like sand dunes, and go on to the pretty village of Fataga.
■ Explore the mountainous interior and the typical inland villages of San Bartolomé de Tirijana or Santa Luciá.

■ Drive round the Tamadaba massif, with its tropical vegetation and rolling mountains.
■ Admire the traditional architecture and wooden balconies in the central village of Teror.

Tenerife

This is the largest island of the group, humid in the north and dry in the south, with a mountain-ous volcanic landscape.

■ Look round the Taganana area of Santa Cruz, the picturesque quarter of the island's capital.
■ Go to La Orotava, with its wooden balconies and a good base to visit the National Park of Las Cañadas del Teide, home to El Pico del Teide, the highest point in Spain at 3 718 metres.
■ See the thousand-year-old Dragon tree in the pretty town of Icod.
■ Stay in the quieter coastal towns such as Los Cristianos or San Juan de La Rambla.

Lanzarote

This barren island is made up of grey ash craters adjacent to some fine beaches.
■ Swim off the beaches of El Reducto, Guacimeta or Playa Blanca of the attractive capital, Arrecife.
■ Drive up to Haria, an oasis town lined with thousands of palm trees.
■ Visit the Cueva de los Verdes, a six-kilometre long volcanic tunnel.

La Palma

This northern island has dramatic black sand beaches and towering mountains.
■ Look around Santa Cruz de la Palma, the capital of this fertile island, with some fine historical buildings around Calle Real and Plaza de España.
■ Take a walk in the Caldera de Taburiente, a National Park of mountainous scenery rising up to 2 400 metres surrounding a massive crater; don't miss the spectacular views from its *miradores*.
■ Drive up to El Roque de los Muchachos, Palma's highest point, through the rugged north of the island which contains unique ecosystems at Los Tilos.

La Gomera

This richly vegetated and exotic island is famed for its inland forests.
■ Walk through Garajonay, a magical National Park of rare laurel forest, declared a UNESCO Heritage Site.
■ Visit Chipude, a small hillside artisans' village below the spectacular Fortaleza de Chipude, a volcanic chimney.

Lanzarote

■ Swim off the volcanic beaches near Valle Gran Rey, a beautiful terraced valley verdant with palm trees.

El Hierro

This is a small and rarely visited island for those who like off-the-beaten-track destinations.
■ Admire the spectacular views of the sea from the *miradores* at La Peña, Jinama or Vascos.
■ Swim in the lava pools of Tornaduste, where there are the island's best beaches.

Fuerteventura

This flat island is best known for some great beaches lining an extensive coastline.
■ Visit the Dunas de Corralejo, a nature reserve with a great expanse of sandy beach.
■ Swim off the great beach at Sotavento or the black-sand beach at Gran Tarajal.
■ Look round the historical town of Betancuría.

Holidays, festivals and events

Thousands of festivals take place each year, most based on the Catholic Church calendar of Saints' Days, though many rites and rituals pre-date Christianity. A large number of local *fiestas* incorporate bull-running and bullfights.

■ **National holidays** January 1; Good Friday; May 1; August 15 (Assumption); October 12 (Spanish Day); November 1 (All Saints); December 6 (Constitution Day); December 25. The calendar can vary slightly each year, and each region has four local holidays to distribute as they wish.

January New Year's Eve is celebrated with seafood meals followed by people swallowing a grape on each stroke of twelve for good luck; Madrid's Puerta del Sol is particularly vibrant. Spanish children get their Christmas presents on January 6th, when the *Reyes Magos* (Three Wise Men) on horse- or even camel-back head noisy and colourful processions in many towns and cities.

February Most towns celebrate carnival time. The rowdiest and most famous *Carnavales* are in Santa Cruz de Tenerife and in Cádiz. There is also a carnival Masked Ball in Madrid.

Holy Week, Seville

March 15–19 *Las Fallas de San José* in Valencia, when huge papier-mâché effigies are constructed and burned on the last day in a ritual to destroy the negativity of the previous year and herald the coming of spring.

April *Semana Santa* or Holy Week is a frenzy of religious celebration all over Spain. The most famous events are in Seville, Málaga, Córdoba and Granada and also in Toledo, Cuenca, Avila, Valladolid and Zamora. Try to catch *La Feria de Sevilla* during the last week in April, with traditional food and drink, Flamenco music and top-name bullfights.

El Rocío, Almonte

May Horse Fair in Jerez. *El Rocío* is a massive Andalusian procession on foot and on horseback to the Hermitage of the Virgin del Rocío in Almonte near Huelva. Other villages similarly honour their local saints. *Fiestas del Dos de Mayo* in Madrid, which celebrate the repulsion of Napoleon's army in 1808.

May 15 *Fiestas de San Isidro*, commemorating Madrid's patron saint, with even more live music, theatre, dance and bullfights.

June Rose petal scattering processions mark the feast of Corpus Christi in many towns, especially vibrant in Toledo, Sevilla, Córdoba, Santiago de Compostela, Avila, Burgos and Valladolid.

July *Sanfermines*, the running of the bulls, in Pamplona. The classical Mérida Theatre Festival is held in the Roman theatre at the end of July/beginning of August. *Bajada de* *la Virgen de las Nieves*, near Santa Cruz, Palma, a religious spectacular occurring every five years.

July 25 The feast of Saint James in the Cathedral of Santiago de Compostela, where his remains are buried.

August International Folk Festival, Los Cristianos, Tenerife.

August 15 A huge feast day celebrating *Nuestra Señora de la Asunción*, especially spectacular at the Basílica de Santa María in Elche (Alicante), where you also see mock battles between Christians and Moors in the same week.

August 16 Hundreds of villages mark the day of San Roque, the patron saint against the plague, particularly in Calatayud (Zaragoza), Llanes (Asturias) and Betanzos (La Coruña).

August 30 In Vilafranca de Penedes (Barcelona) the *Festa Major de Sant Félix* is celebrated with what is considered the best local music and dance in Cataluña.

September San Sebastián Film Festival. The Barcelona International Music Festival begins. Logroño *Festival de la Vendimia*, with wine tasting and bull-running.

September 8 Hundreds of small villages dedicate this day to their patron saint, with music, dancing, fireworks and processions.

October International Film Week in Valladolid.

October 12 *El Día de la Hispanidad*, celebrated throughout the Spanish-speaking world. The *Fiestas del Pilar* are celebrated with most gusto in the Basílica de Nuestra Señora del Pilar, Zaragoza.

November 1 A family celebration honouring All Saints Day.

December Christmas Eve is a family affair with a typical seafood Christmas dinner. Most restaurants close from 9.00 pm and remain closed on Christmas Day.

Bare necessities

Greetings

Hello!	**¡Hola!**
Good morning.	**Buenos días.**
Good afternoon / evening.	**Buenas tardes.**
Good evening / night.	**Buenas noches.**
How are you?	**¿Qué tal?**
Fine, thanks, how are you?	**Muy bien, gracias, ¿y usted?**
See you later.	**Hasta luego.**
See you tomorrow.	**Hasta mañana.**
Bye!	**¡ Adiós!**

Other useful words

Excuse me.	**Por favor, con permiso.**
Sorry.	**¡Perdón!**
Please	**Por favor**
Thank you (very much)	**(Muchas) gracias**
You're welcome.	**De nada.**
Have a good trip!	**¡Buen viaje!**
Have a nice meal!	**¡Que aproveche!**
Here you are.	**Tenga.**
OK	**Muy bien**
It doesn't matter / It's alright.	**No importa.**
Don't worry.	**No se preocupe.**
Of course!	**¡Claro!**
Yes / No	**Sí / No**
Sir / Madam	**Señor / Señora**
Can I (come in)?	**¿Se puede (pasar)?**

Is / are there . . . ?

Is there a telephone?	**¿Hay teléfono?**
Are there any toilets?	**¿Hay servicios?**

Where is / are . . . ?

Where's the station?	**¿Dónde está la estación?**
Where are the shoes?	**¿Dónde están los zapatos?**
Where's the Hotel San Jaime?	**¿Dónde está el Hotel San Jaime?**
It's (on the right / on the left / at the end of the street / 100 metres away).	**Está (a la derecha / a la izquierda / al final de la calle / a cien metros).**

Do you have any . . . ?

Do you have any unleaded petrol?	**¿Tiene gasolina sin plomo?**
Do you have any (prawns)?	**¿Hay (gambas)?**

How much . . . ?

How much is that?	**¿Cuánto es?**
How much does it cost?	**¿Cuánto vale?**
How much are the (strawberries / tomatoes) a kilo?	**¿A cuánto está (las fresas / los tomates) el kilo?**
How much is that altogether?	**¿Cuánto es en total?**

I'd like . . .

I'd like a (shirt / melon).	**Quisiera (una camisa / un melón).**
I'd like a kilo of oranges.	**Deme un kilo de naranjas.**

Getting things straight

Pardon?	**¿Cómo?**
Could you say that again?	**¿Quiere repetir eso?**
More slowly, please.	**Más despacio, por favor.**
I don't understand.	**No entiendo.**
Do you understand?	**¿Entiende?**
How do you write / spell it?	**¿Cómo se escribe?**
Can you write it down, please?	**¿Puede escribirlo, por favor?**
What does it mean?	**¿Qué quiere decir?**
I don't know.	**No sé.**
Is that right?	**¿Verdad?**

About yourself

My name is . . .	**Me llamo . . .**
I'm (Mr / Mrs / Miss) . . .	**Soy (el señor / la señora / la señorita) . . .**
How do you do? / Nice to meet you.	**Encantado/a.**
I'm from . . .	**Soy de . . .**
I'm Irish.	**Soy irlandés/a.**
(see Nationalities p35)	
I live in . . .	**Vivo en . . .**
I study economics.	**Estudio economía.**
I'm a nurse.	**Soy enfermero/a.**
I speak a little Spanish.	**Hablo un poco español.**
I'm here on (holiday / business).	**Estoy aquí de (vacaciones / negocios).**
So am I.	**Yo también.**
I'm staying for a week.	**Paso una semana aquí.**

About other people

What's your name?	**¿Cómo se llama?**
This is (Mr . . . / my husband / my colleague).	**Le presento (al señor . . . / a mi marido / a mi colega).**
This is (Mrs . . . / my wife / my colleague).	**Le presento (a la señora . . . / a mi esposa /a mi colega).**
Where are you from?	**¿De dónde es usted?**
Are you English?	**¿Es usted inglés/a?**
What do you do for a living?	**¿En qué trabaja?**
Do you speak English?	**¿Habla usted inglés?**
Are you here on holidays?	**¿Está usted aquí de vacaciones?**
How long are you staying for?	**¿Cuánto tiempo se queda?**

Money

The currency in Spain is the peseta.

five pesetas	**cinco pesetas (5 ptas)**
twenty-five pesetas	**veinticinco pesetas (25 ptas)**
fifty pesetas	**cincuenta pesetas (50 ptas)**
one hundred pesetas	**cien pesetas (100 ptas)**
one thousand pesetas	**mil pesetas (1.000 ptas)**
(See p34 for all the numbers)	

Changing money

I'd like to change (£100 / $100).	**Quiero cambiar cien (libras / dólares).**
I've got traveller's cheques.	**Tengo cheques de viaje.**
Here you are.	**Aquí tiene.**
What is the exchange rate?	**¿A cómo está el cambio?**
What is the pound at?	**¿A cuánto está la libra?**
The pound is at 200 pesetas.	**La libra está a doscientas pesetas.**
What's the commission charge?	**¿Cuánto es la comisión?**
¿Puedo ver su pasaporte?	Can I see your passport?
La comisión es . . .	The commission charge is . . .

The time

What time is it?	**¿Qué hora es?**
It's (midday / midnight).	**Es mediodía / medianoche.**
It's one o'clock.	**Es la una.**
It's (two / three / four) o'clock.	**Son las (dos / tres / cuatro).**
It's five past ten in the morning.	**Son las diez y cinco de la mañana.**
It's quarter past three in the afternoon.	**Son las tres y cuarto de la tarde.**
At half past seven in the evening.	**A las siete y media de la tarde.**
At twenty to nine in the morning.	**A las siete menos veinte de la mañana.**
At quarter to eleven at night.	**A las once menos cuarto de la noche.**
What time do you (open / close)?	**¿A qué hora (abren / cierran)?**
What time does it (leave / arrive)?	**¿A qué hora (sale / llega)?**
At nine thirty in the morning.	**A las nueve y media de la mañana.**

Alphabet

In Spanish the letters of the alphabet are pronounced as follows.

A (ah)	**H** (achay)	**N** (ehnay)	**T** (tay)
B (bay)	**I** (ee)	**Ñ** (ehnyay)	**U** (oo)
C (thay)	**J** (chota)	**O** (oh)	**V** (uvay)
D (day)	**K** (ka)	**P** (pay)	**W** (ubay doblay)
E (eh)	**L** (ehlay)	**Q** (koo)	**X** (ekees)
F (ehffay)	**LL** (ehyay)	**R** (ehrray)	**Y** (eegreeayga)
G (chay)	**M** (ehmay)	**S** (ehssay)	**Z** (thaytah)

Numbers

0	cero	70	setenta
1	un/uno/una*	80	ochenta
2	dos	90	noventa
3	tres	100	cien
4	cuatro	101	ciento uno
5	cinco	110	ciento diez
6	seis	200	doscientos
7	siete	293	doscientos
8	ocho		noventa y tres
9	nueve	300	trescientos
10	diez	400	cuatrocientos
11	once	500	quinientos
12	doce	600	seiscientos
13	trece	700	setecientos
14	catorce	800	ochocientos
15	quince	900	novecientos
16	dieciséis	1.000	mil
17	diecisiete	1.047	mil cuarenta y
18	dieciocho		siete**
19	diecinueve	2.000	dos mil
20	veinte	2.380	dos mil
21	veintiuno		trescientos
22	veintidós		ochenta**
23	veintitrés	3.000	tres mil
24	veinticuatro	1.000.000	un millón**
25	veinticinco	1.675.834	un millón seis-
26	veintiséis		cientos seten-
27	veintisiete		ta y cinco mil,
28	veintiocho		ochocientos
29	veintinueve		treinta y
30	treinta		cuatro
40	cuarenta		
50	cincuenta		
60	sesenta		

* **el número uno** = number one; **un sombrero** = a hat; **una naranja** = an orange; ** In Spanish numbers, full stops, not commas, are used after thousands and millions,
eg 1.047   2.3801.000.000   1.675.834

Ordinal numbers

1st	primero/a	7th	séptimo/a
2nd	segundo/a	8th	octavo/a
3rd	tercero/a	9th	noveno/a
4th	cuarto/a	10th	décimo/a
5th	quinto/a	11th	undécimo/a
6th	sexto/a	12th	duodécimo/a

Countries and nationalities

America	**America / Norteamérica: americano/a /norteamericano/a**
Argentina	**Argentina: argentino/a**
Australia	**Australia: australiano/a**
Austria	**Austria: austriaco/a**
Belgium	**Bélgica: belga**
Brazil	**Brasil: brasileño/a**
Canada	**Canadá: canadiense**
Chile	**chile: chileno/a**
China	**China: chino/a**
Denmark	**Dinamarca: danés/danesa**
England	**Inglaterra: inglés/esa**
Finland	**Finlandia: finlandés/esa**
France	**Francia: francés/esa**
Germany	**Alemania: alemán/a**
Greece	**Grecia: griego/a**
Hong Kong	**Hong Kong: hong konés/konesa**
India	**la India: hindú**
Iraq	**Irak: iraquí**
Ireland	**Irlanda: irlandés/esa**
Italy	**Italia: italiano/a**
Japan	**Japón: japonés/esa**
Luxembourg	**Luxemburgo: luxemburgués/esa**
Mexico	**México: mexicano/a**
Morocco	**Marruecos: marroquí**
Netherlands / Holland	**los Países Bajos / Holanda: holandés/esa**
New Zealand	**Nueva Zelanda: neocelandés/esa**
Northern Ireland	**Irlanda del Norte: irlandés/a**
Norway	**Noruega: noruego/a**
Portugal	**Portugal: portugués/esa**
Russia	**Rusia: ruso/a**
Scotland	**Escocia: escocés/esa**
South Africa	**Sudáfrica / Suráfrica: sudafricano/a / surafricano/a**
Spain	**España: español/a**
Sweden	**Suecia: sueco/a**
Switzerland	**Suiza: suizo/a**
United States	**los Estados Unidos: estadounidense/a / americano/ a**
Wales	**Gales: galés/a**

Days

Monday	**lunes**	the day before yesterday	**anteayer**
Tuesday	**martes**		
Wednesday	**miércoles**	tomorrow	**mañana**
Thursday	**jueves**	the day after tomorrow	**pasado mañana**
Friday	**viernes**		
Saturday	**sábado**	last (Thursday)	**el (jueves) pasado**
Sunday	**domingo**		
today	**hoy**	next (Wednesday)	**el (miércoles) que viene**
yesterday	**ayer**		

Months

January	**enero**	July	**julio**
February	**febrero**	August	**agosto**
March	**marzo**	September	**setiembre**
April	**abril**	October	**octubre**
May	**mayo**	November	**noviembre**
June	**junio**	December	**diciembre**

Dates

the first of (January)	**el primero de (enero)**
the (second / third) of (February / March)	**el (dos / tres) de (febrero / marzo)**

Seasons

spring	**la primavera**
summer	**el verano**
autumn	**el otoño**
winter	**el invierno**

Colours

black	**negro/a**	orange	**naranja**
blue	**azul**	red	**rojo/a**
brown	**marrón**	white	**blanco/a**
green	**verde**	yellow	**amarillo/a**

Sound Check

c
When **c** is followed by the letter **e** or **i** it is pronounced like the 'th' in 'thin'.

cebolla	theboya
cinco	theenko

Practise with these words:
cien, cincuenta, catorce, doce, despacio

Language works

At the market

1 Buying tomatoes at the market
- ■ **Buenas tardes.**
- □ **Buenas tardes. ¿Hay tomates?**
- ■ **Sí, claro.**
- □ **Déme dos kilos.**
- ■ **Dos kilos.**
- □ **¿Cuánto es?**
- ■ **Ciento diez pesetas.**
- □ **Gracias, adiós.**
- ■ **Adiós, buenas tardes.**

Is it morning or afternoon?
How much are tomatoes a kilo?

Changing money

2 Pounds for pesetas
- ■ **Buenos días.**
- □ **Buenos días. ¿A cuánto está la libra?**
- ■ **Está a ciento ochenta y cinco pesetas.**
- □ **Quiero cambiar veinticinco libras.**
- ■ **Muy bien. El pasaporte, por favor.**

How much would you get, about, for your £25?
What does the assistant ask you for?

Try it out

What do you say when . . .

1 you're desperate to go to the toilet?
2 you greet somebody in the afternoon?
3 you want to know what time a shop opens?
4 you want to get past somebody in a supermarket?
5 you want to know where your hotel (the Hotel San Jorge) is?
6 you want somebody to repeat something?
7 you want to know if they have unleaded petrol?
8 you want to know how much to pay?

As if you were there

You're looking for a bank in Cádiz.
You see a lady walking by.
- ■ (Say excuse me)
- □ She stops
- ■ (Say good morning)
- □ **Buenos días.**
- ■ (Ask where the bank is)
- □ **Al final de esta calle.**
- ■ (Ask what time it closes)
- □ **A las dos de la tarde.**
- ■ (Thank her)
- □ **De nada, adiós.**
- ■ (Say goodbye)

Getting around

Santa Justa station, Seville

Arrival points

By air
International flights from most
countries arrive at Madrid and
Barcelona. There are also regular
flights serving Alicante, Bilbao,
Gran Canaria, Málaga, Palma de
Mallorca, Santiago de Compostela,
Sevilla, Tenerife, Valencia,
Valladolid and Zaragoza. Charter
flights go to other destinations,
especially during high season.
Wherever you fly to you will find it
easy to catch onward bus or rail
services to most towns. All airports
have regular bus services to the
nearest town centres and taxis are
usually a reasonably cheap option.
You can hire cars at every airport.

By road
Madrid lies at the geographical
centre of Spain and all major N
(National) roads start radially from
there. Spain has invested heavily in
new roads – especially along the
Mediterranean coast, around
Madrid and internal routes to
international borders – so it is worth

getting an up-to-date road map. On
some of the newest motorways
(*autopistas*), you pay a toll (*peaje*).
There are plenty of petrol and
service stations with restaurants and
shops along the way.

If you bring your own car, get a
green card from your insurance
company before you leave the
country.

IBERPISTAS. S. A.		
AUTOPISTA [A-6]		
VILLALBA - VILLACASTIN - ADANERO		

TARIFAS DE PEAJE			
		TRAMOS	
CATEGORIAS	PEAJE ENTRE VILLALBA Y VILLACASTIN	PEAJE ENTRE VILLACASTIN Y ADANERO	PEAJE RECORRIDO COMPLETO
MOTOS TURISMOS FURGONES R/ SENC. TUR. CON REMOLQUE	725	230	330
FURGONES R/ DOBLES CAMIONES 2/3 EJES AUTOBUSES MICROBUSES	1940	480	645
CAMIONES DE MAS DE 3 EJES	2190	525	710

Travelling around Spain

Car/motorbike hire

Hiring a car or motorbike is expensive if you do it locally once you arrive in Spain. It can be up to 40% cheaper if you hire the car through a travel agent in your own country, so check out fly-drive options before you book your flight. In tourist areas, you may find smaller, independent operators much cheaper than the international names. Big-name car hire companies are represented at all main airports and train stations. You will need to show your passport, a clean driving licence and must be over 21 with at least a year's experience. You can hire an under 75cc moped at 14, but you must be over 18 to hire anything bigger. Helmets are compulsory.

Spain has one of the highest accident rates in Europe, so take care especially at night (drink driving is a big problem). Parking and congestion are a problem in larger cities, where thefts from cars are common. Never leave any visible belongings when you park. Watch out also for wheel clampers; being clamped means a hefty fine and lots of paperwork.

! I'd like to hire a car.
Quisiera alquilar un coche.

Road travel at a glance

■ *Autopistas*: fast two-, three- or four-lane motorways, often with a toll.

■ *Autovías*: much the same as *autopistas*, but without a toll.
■ N roads and *Carreteras comarcales*: national main roads and local roads are main roads with two-way traffic; some of these have sections with *carácter de autovía*, with speed limits and regulations to match *autovías*.
Speed limits 50 kmh in built-up areas; 90 kmh on roads outside built-up areas ; 100 kmh on dual carriageways and 120 kmh on motorways. Remember seatbelts are compulsory. Hidden radar traps are common on main roads and police can demand large on-the-spot fines for speeding.

Petrol This is moderately-priced. Petrol stations selling leaded or unleaded petrol are prevalent throughout Spain, and most accept credit cards. In remote areas, you may need to pay by cash.
Breakdowns There are special SOS phones on *autopistas* and *autovías* to call for help if you break down. Otherwise dial 192. If you are a member of an automobile club, check to see if it has a reciprocal agreement with RACE (*Real Automóvil Club de España*), which can be contacted on (91 – from outside Madrid) 447 3200.
For information about a particular route, phone 900 123 505.

! Fill up with unleaded, please.
Llénelo de gasolina sin plomo.

Aire y Agua

```
Próximas LLegadas              Próximas Salidas
Regionales y L. Recorrido      Cercanías        Regionales y L. Recorrido
H.Prev. Procedencia  Via   Hora  Destino  Via  Hora  Destino  Via  Tren

13:10 BADAJ/CACER 5        13:10 FUENLABRADA 9   13:10 BARCELONA 5 TALGO
13:19 JAEN                       MOSTOL/SOTO 8   13:33 AVILA      2 REGIO
13:46 TOLEDO     4               PARLA        6  13:50 ALBACETE   5 R EXP
13:49 CARTAGENA           13:05 P PIO/VILLA  7   14:00 SEGOVIA    2 REGIO
14:15 SANTANDER  5        13:10 CHAMARTIN    2   14:15 ALICANTE   5 TALGO
14:20 ALICANTE   5        13:10 ALCALA       3   14:20 GIJON      5 TALGO
                         13:13 TRES CANTOS   2   14:25 TOLEDO     4 REGIO
                         13:16 COSLADA           15:03 SEGOVIA    2 REGIO
                         13:22 GUADALAJARA   3
                         13:23 CHAMAR/P PI   2
```

By rail

International rail routes from France go to San Sebastián and Madrid or to Barcelona, with onward connections to most other main cities. There are smaller border crossings through the Pyrenees to Cataluña and Aragón (often involving a change of train). From Portugal, main routes are from Lisbon to Madrid or from Porto to Galicia.

The main Spanish rail system is the state-run RENFE. Understanding the types of train service and prices is a complicated business, and there are all kinds of special discounts available on certain days (*Días Azules*) or for groups.

Types of train include *cercanías* (local/commuter trains), *trenes regionales* (provincial trains) and the faster *trenes de largo recorrido* or *Electrotrén* (long-distance trains), which may be an *expreso* or the faster *rápido*. The fastest options are the Intercity *Talgo* or *Pendular* trains, though there are differing degrees of comfort, price and journey times, depending on the route and time you want to travel. The *Talgo* trains have air-conditioning, piped music, sleeping compartments and the option of a video! These more luxurious trains cost up to 60% more; check what you are paying for with station staff who are usually helpful.

Tickets

Buy your ticket at the ticket office or from automatic machines before you board your train, or you are liable to a fine. Children between four and eleven are eligible for a discount of 40%, depending on the route, while toddlers under three travel for free.

! A return ticket, please.
Un billete de ida y vuelta.

Passes

Tarjeta Turística, a first or second-class rail pass available to any non-Spanish resident, which allows unlimited travel for three to ten days.
Eurodomino Pass, provides three, five or ten day's travel within a month on the Spanish network, but must be bought in the country of origin.
Inter-Rail Pass, allows EU citizens under 26 unlimited travel for one month, but must also be bought in your own country.
Group discounts If you are travelling in a group of ten or more, you can get a 40% discount.
Senior citizens You are entitled to discount on Spanish trains if you obtain a REX card from your own country.

Special trains and lines

FEVE, a conglomeration of small
private companies that run a series
of shorter routes not covered by
RENFE, especially in out-of-the-
way tourist areas such as the north
western tip of Galicia and along the
Cantabrian coast, from El Ferrol to
Bilbao and Santander. This is a
scenic route but services can be
sporadic.
AVE, the high-speed train which
links Madrid to Seville in under three
hours.
Expreso Al-Andalus From April to
December, this Spanish 'Orient
Express' offers a five-day tour of
the Andalusian cities of Seville,
Córdoba, Granada, Málaga and
Jerez de la Frontera. The price of the
ticket on this luxurious train includes
meals and entertainment in the most
exclusive restaurants and clubs in
each city.
El tren de la naturaleza This scenic
train runs from Cercedilla in the
Madrid Sierra up a pine-forested
mountain, with stops at villages and
ski resorts.
El tren de la fresa, a steam train
which runs from Madrid to Aranjuez
(see p8).

Coaches

Coaches are a reliable way of travelling, often working out faster and no
more expensive than local trains.
There are hundreds of independent
coach firms providing reasonably-
priced services all over Spain.

There are regular international
connections by coach to Madrid,
Barcelona and other main resorts.
Long-distance coaches (*autocares*) are
quite fast with air-conditioning and
videos. Buy your ticket at the office
before boarding for longer journeys.
In smaller towns or on shorter
journeys, you usually pay on boarding. Local buses are efficient and
generally reliable, though check
timetables carefully in rural or non-
tourist areas, as there may be only
one bus a day passing through.
Sundays and holidays (*festivos*) may
have extremely reduced services.

What time does the bus to
Sevilla leave?
**¿A qué hora sale el autocar
para Sevilla?**

Ferries

International ferry connections link
Bilbao and Santander with Britain in
the north; and there are services
from Algeciras and Tarifa to
Morocco in the south (with
additional seasonal hydrofoils and
ferries to Melilla and Tangier from
Almería, Benalmadena and
Málaga). For the Balearic Islands,
there are ferry connections with
Barcelona, Valencia and Denia.

City transport

Metro and RENFE
cercanías tickets

Buy metro tickets at the ticket office in each station, or from the automatic machine. Buy *un billete sencillo* for one journey or a ten-trip ticket (*un billete de diez*), both carrying magnetic strips. Entry barriers are automatic; insert your ticket arrow first (a display will show you how many trips you have left on a ten-trip ticket) and go through the turnstile. Don't forget to pick up your ticket on the other side; travelling without a valid ticket could get you a fine. *Cercanías* tickets can be bought at station ticket offices.

❗ A ten-trip ticket, please.
¿Me da un billete de diez?

Buses
Pay the driver for single journeys, or buy a more economical ten-trip card in *estancos* (tobacconist's) or *quioscos* (newspaper kiosks). You can get a free city bus-route map from tourist offices, though routes are clearly shown on bus stops.
See pp7 and 11 for more details on Madrid and Barcelona.

❗ Are there buses to Zamora?
¿Hay autobuses para Zamora?

Taxis
Taxis are relatively inexpensive, though you can be charged extra at night, weekends and on holidays. Each taxi driver should have a list of approved fares for trips to stations, airports and main sites.

Phrasemaker

Asking the way

Excuse me . . .	**Perdone, por favor . . .**
Which way is (the market / the station), please?	**¿(El mercado / la estación), por favor?**
Is (the cathedral / the market) near here?	**¿Está por aquí (la catedral / el mercado)?**
Is there (a bank / a chemist's) near here?	**¿Hay (un banco / una farmacia) por aquí?**

Allí está	There it is
A la (derecha / izquierda)	To the (right / left)
Todo recto	Straight on
La (primera / segunda / tercera) a la (derecha / izquierda)	The (first / second / third) on the (right / left)
Cruce el puente	Cross the bridge
En la esquina	On the corner
A cien metros	100 metres away
Al final de la calle	At the end of the street
(bastante) Lejos	A (fairly) long way away

Places to look for

English	Spanish	English	Spanish
beach	**la playa**	railway station	**la estación del ferrocarril**
bus station	**la estación de autobuses**	square	**la plaza**
castle	**el castillo**	main square	**la plaza mayor**
cathedral	**la catedral**	stadium	**el estadio**
(town) centre	**el centro (ciudad)**	store	**el comercio**
chemist's	**una farmacia**	street	**la calle**
church	**la iglesia**	swimming pool	**la piscina**
market	**el mercado**	toilets	**los servicios / los lavabos**
museum	**el museo**	Tourist Office	**la Oficina de Turismo**
palace	**el palacio**	Town Hall	**el Ayunta- miento**
park	**el parque**	walls (of a town)	**la muralla**
port	**el puerto**		
Post Office	**Correos**		
shop	**la tienda**		

Hiring a car or bike

A hire car	**Un coche de alquiler**
I'd like to hire (a car / a bike).	**Quisiera alquilar (un coche / una bicicleta).**
A small car	**Un coche pequeño**
A fairly big car	**Un coche bastante grande**
For three days.	**Para tres días.**
Is insurance included?	**¿Está incluido el seguro?**
Unlimited mileage?	**¿Kilometraje ilimitado?**
How much is it?	**¿Cuánto es?**

¿Qué tipo?	What type?
Tenemos . . .	We have . . .
Ocho mil pesetas al día	Eight thousand pesetas a day
Cuarenta y cinco mil pesetas a la semana	Forty-five thousand pesetas a week
Su permiso de conducir	Your driving licence

Buying petrol

Is it self-service?	**¿Es autoservicio?**
30 litres of (4-star / unleaded)	**Treinta litros de (súper / gasolina sin plomo)**
Fill up with unleaded please.	**Llénelo de gasolina sin plomo.**
Do you have (air / water / oil)?	**¿Tienen (aire / agua / aceite)?**

Checking where you are

Is Cuenca far?	**¿Está lejos Cuenca?**
How far is Cuenca?	**¿A cuántos kilómetros está Cuenca?**
(See Numbers p34)	
Is this the road to Segovia?	**¿Es ésta la carretera de Segovia?**
Where is Trujillo?	**¿Dónde está Trujillo?**

Using the underground

A single ticket, please.	**Un billete de ida.**
A ten-trip ticket, please.	**¿Me da un billete de diez?**
Does this train go to Callao?	**¿Va este tren a Callao?**
What line is Sol on?	**¿En qué línea está Sol?**
Is the next stop Gracia?	**¿La próxima parada es Gracia?**

Getting information on trains and buses

Are there buses to . . .?	**¿Hay autobuses para . . .?**
Are there trains to . . .?	**¿Hay trenes para . . .?**
What time does (the bus / the train) to Seville leave?	**¿A qué hora sale (el autobús / el tren) para Sevilla?**
What time does the next one leave? (See the Time p33)	**¿A qué hora sale el próximo?**
Which platform does it leave from?	**¿De qué andén sale?**
What time does it arrive?	**¿A qué hora llega?**
How long does it take?	**¿Cuánto tarda?**
Do you have a timetable?	**¿Tiene un horario?**

Buying a ticket

Where is the ticket office?	**¿Dónde está la taquilla?**
A return ticket, please.	**Un billete de ida y vuelta.**
A single ticket, please.	**Un billete de ida solo.**
Two adults and one child	**Dos adultos y un niño**
Smoking / Non-smoking	**Fumador / No fumador**

Catching a taxi

Is there a taxi rank?	**¿Hay una parada de taxis?**
The airport, please.	**Al aeropuerto, por favor.**
Is it far?	**¿Está lejos?**
Could I have a receipt?	**¿Me da un recibo?**
How much is it?	**¿Cuánto cuesta?**
Here you are.	**Tenga.**

A media hora, más o menos	About half an hour
Está a tres kilometros, más o menos.	It's about three kilometres, more or less.

Language works

Asking your way

1 A passer-by helps you get to the castle
- **¿El castillo, por favor?**
- □ **Está al final de la calle, a la izquierda.**

The castle is at … on the right/left

Hiring a car

2 You hire a car
- **Quisiera alquilar un coche.**
- □ **¿Qué tipo?**
- **Un coche pequeño.**
- □ **Tenemos el Ford Fiesta y el Seat Ibiza, a siete mil quinientas pesetas al día.**
- **El Ibiza, por favor.**

They will have to pay ….. a day.

Getting petrol and checking where you are

3 Getting close to Avila
- **Buenos días, treinta litros de gasolina sin plomo.**
- □ **Muy bien. ¿Algo más?**
- **No, gracias. ¿A cuántos kilómetros está Avila?**
- □ **A treinta kilómetros, más o menos.**
- **Gracias, adiós.**
- (**¿Algo más?** = Anything else?)

How far is it to Avila?

Getting information on trains and buses

4 Toledo and back by train
- **¿Hay trenes para Toledo?**
- □ **Sí, a las once veinte y a las trece diez.**
- **¿De qué andén sale?**
- □ **Número nueve.**
- **¿Cuánto tarda?**
- □ **Veinte minutos.**
- **Deme un billete de ida y vuelta.**

Trains to Toledo are at ….. and …..
They leave from platform …..
Journey time …..

Catching a taxi

5 A quick trip to the Prado museum
- **Buenos días, ¿está lejos el Museo del Prado?**
- □ **No, a cinco minutos, más o menos … … El Museo del Prado**
- **¿Cuánto es?**
- □ **Seiscientas cincuenta.**
- **Muy bien.**
- □ **Gracias, adiós.**

The price of the journey was more / less than 500 pesetas.

Sound Check

q
q is always followed by **u** in Spanish and together the sound is like the 'k' in 'kick'.

aquí	akee
alquilar	alkeelar

Practise with these words:
qué, pequeño, quinientas, izquierda, quisiera.

ll
This sound in Spanish is very different from the 'l' in English. It is similar to the 'gh' sound in 'higher' and sounds almost like a 'y'.

billete	beeyehteh
calle	kaiyeh

Practise with these words:
lleno, castillo, taquilla, sencillo, muralla

Try it out

Picture this

Match the picture with the word or phrase.

a **A la izquierda**
b **Farmacia**
c **Un tren grande**
d **A las once y media**
e **Servicios**
f **A la derecha**

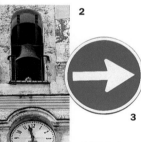

Crossed lines

In each of these conversations, put the lines in the most logical order.

1
☐ **La primera a la izquierda.**
■ **Gracias.**
■ **¿Está lejos?**
■ **¿La estación del ferrocarril, por favor?**
☐ **No, a unos setecientos metros.**

2
☐ **A las nueve treinta.**
☐ **Andén cinco.**
☐ **Gracias.**
■ **¿A qué hora sale el tren para Valencia?**
■ **¿De qué andén?**

As if you were there

In the Information Office, you ask about getting to Salamanca.
■ (Ask if there are buses to Salamanca)
☐ **Sí, hay autobuses y trenes.**
■ (Ask when the bus leaves)
☐ **A las nueve, las once y las diecisiete.**
■ (Ask how long it takes)
☐ **Dos horas y media.**
■ (Order two return tickets)

47

Somewhere to stay

There is a wide range of accommodation available, from hotels and apartments to more unusual options like hidden-away farmhouses or even castles and monasteries. If you have time, it is worth contacting your Spanish Tourist Board about the following options several months in advance to check what is available and get the pick of the best.

It is usually more economical to book in advance through a travel agent, especially deals that include flight and accommodation with optional car hire. If you hire a car, check that there are parking facilities available. Remember that the summer months are the most hectic, and that most coastal resorts will be packed.

Types of accommodation

Self-catering Eating out is relatively cheap and fun so self-catering does not necessarily work out that much cheaper. However, if booked in advance, you could pick a fine villa or apartment in the destination of your choice, a good option if you have a large family or group. *Apartamentos* can be rented independently, or as part of a tourist hotel complex with or without self-catering facilities or maid service.

Paradores Nacionales These are luxury state-run hotels in some of the most impressive beauty spots, often in converted historic buildings such as castles or monasteries, where you dine in style in ancient banqueting halls or medieval refectories. Well worth at least one night if you can afford it.

Hotels These range in quality from one to five stars, and once above three stars you can be sure of fairly good-quality accommodation.

Hostales These are graded from one to three stars. One-star *hostales* are simple, but most *hostales* offer good clean rooms, usually with bathroom en suite, often with a restaurant service too.

Hostales Residenciales These are much the same as *Hostales*, without the restaurant but usually with a bar/cafeteria attached to offer breakfast if required.

Do you have a room?
¿Tienen una habitación libre?

Pensiones and Casas de Huéspedes These tend to be more modest places, though usually clean and well run by the owner and his/her family. You can request meals, too.

Conventos and Monasterios
These are an option if you want peace and tranquility. You may sleep in cheap basic cells, but the settings are often unbelievably beautiful, particularly in Galicia, Catalonia and Mallorca. Check in local tourist offices or telephone in advance, but they are usually so out of the way that it should be possible just to turn up.

Casas Rurales These are little-known options for people who want to get away from it all. You can often rent a small cottage attached to a farm or a house in a wonderful country setting. You can sometimes get horse-riding, fishing or other facilities thrown in.

Balnearios (Health Spas) Pamper yourself in some of the most beautiful mountain settings in Spain. Several date from Roman times and many boast incredible architecture and decoration. The tourist board can give details of those you can stay in.

Campsites There are over 800 official campsites concentrated particularly on the coast, most with good facilities. Camping wild is permitted but check regulations with tourist offices, or locally before pitching your tent.

❗ Are we allowed to camp here?
¿Se puede acampar aquí?

Youth Hostels These are rarely cheaper than sharing a room in a cheap *pensión*. Most are found in the north. Technically you need a YHA card for access.

Refugios These are run in mountain areas for trekkers by the Federación Española de Montañismo. They are very rudimentary with basic kitchen facilities and bunks.

❗ Do you have space for a caravan?
¿Tienen sitio para una caravana?

Children

Children are made very welcome in Spain and most types of accommodation cater for children of all ages, but it is advisable to check beforehand if possible, especially if you tend to stay in smaller *pensiones* or if the children are very young. Cots can usually be arranged if the hotel is notified in advance.

Booking when you get there

If you decide to book on arriving at your destination in Spain, remember the following points:

■ Try places off the main tourist track first if you have transport. If you are in a town and dependent on public transport, go a few blocks from the main train/bus terminal before you look for a place and you will get a better deal.

■ Check the legal price list on show in each establishment, detailing prices for low, mid and high season, for singles/doubles with/without bathroom/shower/en suite and so on. If you have problems with your room or feel you have been unfairly charged, ask for the *libro de reclamaciones*, inspected regularly by the police. By law, the hotelier must produce it if you want to write a complaint.

■ You may request an extra bed for your room, which carries a maximum surcharge of 35% above the indicated price of a double room, 60% of the price of a single.

■ You will usually have to leave your passport as security until you have paid the bill.

■ Do not leave money or valuables in your room.

❗ Your passport, please.
El pasaporte, por favor.

Phrasemaker

Places to stay

hotel	**un hotel**
boarding house	**una pensión / una casa de huéspedes**
bed (and breakfast)	**camas**
campsite	**un camping**
flat to let	**un apartamento de alquiler**

Finding a place

Do you have a room?	**¿Tienen una habitación libre?**
A single room	**Una habitación individual**
A double room	**Una habitación doble**
For (three) people	**Para (tres) personas**
For (two) nights	**Para (dos) noches**
For a weekend	**Para un fin de semana**
Can I see the room?	**¿Puedo ver la habitación?**
How much is the room?	**¿Cuánto cuesta la habitación?**
We'll see.	**Ya veremos.**
We'll take it.	**La tomamos.**

¿Para cuántas noches?	How many nights?
¿Para cuántas personas?	How many people?
Lo siento.	I'm sorry.
Está todo completo.	We're full.
Los niños a mitad de precio	Children half-price

Specifications

Does it have (a bathroom / a shower / a child's bed)?	**¿Tiene (baño / ducha / cama de niño)?**
With a (single / double) bed	**Con cama (individual / de matrimonio)**
With (two) beds	**Con (dos) camas**
Is breakfast included?	**¿Está incluido el desayuno?**
How much is (full board / half board)?	**¿Cuánto es (la pensión completa / la media pensión)?**
El desayuno es aparte.	Breakfast is separate.
No tenemos camas de matrimonio.	We don't have any double beds.

Checking in and getting information

I have a reservation . . .	**Tengo una reserva . . .**
. . . in the name of Brindley	**. . . a nombre de Brindley**
Where can I park?	**¿Dónde puedo aparcar?**
What floor is it on?	**¿En qué piso está?**
Where's (the lift / the staircase)?	**¿Dónde está (el ascensor / la escalera)?**
What time is (breakfast / dinner)?	**¿A qué hora es (el desayuno / la cena)?**
Is there (a lift / air conditioning)?	**¿Hay (ascensor / aire acondicionado)?**

(El nombre / El pasaporte), por favor.	(Your name / Your passport), please.
¿Quiere rellenar la ficha?	Please fill in the form

Habitación número . . .	Room number . . .
Es el número (trescientos veinte)	It's number (three hundred and twenty)
Está en el tercer piso.	It's on the third floor.
La escalera está (a mano derecha / a la derecha).	The stairs are on the right.
El ascensor está (a mano izquierda / a la izquierda).	The lift is on the left.
Desde las siete y media hasta las diez	From 7.30 to 10.00
	(See Times p33)
¿La matrícula de su coche?	Your car registration number?
¿Va(n) a cenar?	Are you going to have dinner?
Aquí está la llave.	Here's the key.

In your room

bathroom	**el cuarto de baño**
bed	**la cama**
blind	**la persiana**
bulb	**la bombilla**
door	**la puerta**
fridge/mini-bar	**la nevera/el mini bar**
iron	**la plancha**
lamp	**la lámpara**
light switch	**el interruptor de la luz**
lock	**la cerradura**
phone	**el teléfono**
price-list – on back of door	**la tarifa**
shower	**la ducha**
tap	**el grifo**
television	**la televisión**
towel	**la toalla**
washbasin	**el lavabo**
window	**la ventana**

Asking for help

Could you call me at eight?	**¿Me llaman a las ocho?**
Do you have a safe?	**¿Tienen una caja fuerte?**
(The television / The telephone) isn't working.	**(La televisión / El teléfono) no funciona.**
There's no (hot water / toilet paper).	**No hay (agua caliente / papel higiénico).**
There are no (pillows / blankets).	**No hay (almohadas / mantas).**
How does (the blind / the shower) work?	**¿Cómo funciona (la persiana / la ducha)?**
Do you have an iron?	**¿Tienen una plancha?**

Ahora viene alguien.	There's somebody coming.
Se aprieta este botón.	You press this button.

53

Paying

I'd like to pay the bill.	**Quiero pagar la cuenta.**
by (credit card / traveller's cheque)	**con (tarjeta de crédito / cheques de viaje)**
by cash	**en metálico**
I think there's a mistake.	**Creo que hay un error.**

¿Qué número de habitación?	What room number?
La llave, por favor.	The key, please.
¿Cómo va a pagar?	How are you going to pay?
¡Buen viaje!	Have a good trip!
Firme aquí.	Sign here, please.

(El coche / la tienda / la caravana) cuesta . . . pesetas al día.	(The car / the tent / the caravan) costs . . . pesetas a day.

Campsites

Do you have space for (a car / a motor-bike / a caravan)?	**¿Tienen sitio para (un coche / una moto / una caravana)?**
How much is it?	**¿Cuánto cuesta?**
Where are (the showers / the dustbins / the toilets)?	**¿Dónde están (las duchas / los cubos de la basura / los servicios)?**
Is there (a shop / a laundry / a swimming pool)?	**¿Hay (tienda / lavandería / piscina)?**

Sound Check

b and v
b and **v** are pronounced in the same way, just like 'b' in English.

va	ba
baño	banyo

Practise with these words:
viene, van, habitación, nombre, ver, veinte, buen

Language works

Finding a place

1 You get a room for two
- **Buenas tardes**
- □ **Buenas tardes. ¿Tienen una habitación libre?**
- **¿Una habitación doble?**
- □ **Sí, doble.**
- **¿Para cuántas noches?**
- □ **Una noche.**
- **Muy bien.**
- □ **¿Cuánto cuesta?**
- **Nueve mil pesetas la habitación.**

How much is your double room?

Specifications

2 You check what is available in your double room
- **¿Tiene ducha la habitación?**
- □ **Todas las habitaciones tienen baño con ducha.**
- **Bien. Y ¿tiene cama de matrimonio?**
- □ **No, son dos camas individuales.**

You get a shower: true/false?
You'll be sleeping in a double bed:
true/false?

Checking prices

3 Your reservation turns out OK
- **Tengo una reserva a nombre de Westwood.**
- □ **Muy bien, un momento, por favor . . . sí, Westwood, una habitación individual para dos noches.**
- **¿Cuánto cuesta la habitación?**
- □ **Siete mil trescientas pesetas.**
- **¿Está incluido el desayuno?**
- □ **No, el desayuno cuesta setecientas cincuenta.**
- **Muy bien.**
- □ **El pasaporte, por favor. Y ¿quiere rellenar esta ficha?**

What will you pay for two nights' bed and breakfast?
What two things do you have to do next?

Finding your way around

4 You find out where things are
- **Es la habitación número cuatrocientos sesenta y siete, en el segundo piso.**
- □ **Gracias. ¿Hay ascensor?**
- **Sí, aquí a la izquierda.**
- □ **Gracias. Y ¿dónde está el restaurante?**
- **Está en el primer piso.**

You sleep on the ..... floor and eat on the ..... floor.

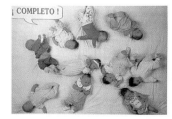

¡ COMPLETO !

Finding out meal-times

5 You plan when and what to eat
- Por favor, ¿a qué hora es el desayuno?
- ☐ Desde las ocho hasta las diez y media. Y ¿van a cenar?
- ¿A qué hora es la cena?
- ☐ Desde las nueve hasta las once y media.
- Sí.

What's the earliest time for breakfast? and for dinner?

Asking for help

6 The porter helps you out
- Por favor, ¿cómo funciona la televisión?
- ☐ Se aprieta este botón. (He shows you)
- Gracias. Y no hay agua caliente en el cuarto de baño.
- ☐ No, hay un problema con el agua. Ahora viene alguien.
- Gracias.
- ☐ De nada.

Will you be getting help?

Paying

7 You check out and settle up
- Quiero pagar la cuenta.
- ☐ Muy bien. ¿Qué número de habitación tiene?
- La cuatrocientas sesenta y siete.
- ☐ Pues son quince mil ochocientas cincuenta y nueve, todo incluido. ¿Cómo va a pagar?
- Con tarjeta de crédito.
- ☐ Muy bien . . . ¿quiere firmar aquí? . . . Gracias. Adiós y ¡buen viaje!

You pay less than 20.000 pesetas: true/false?
They accept your credit card first time: true/false?

At the campsite

8 Finding space for your caravan
- ¿Tienen sitio para una caravana?
- ☐ Sí, ¿para cuántas noches?
- Una noche. ¿Cuánto cuesta?
- ☐ Dos mil pesetas el coche y el remolque.
- ¿Hay piscina?
- ☐ Sí, claro.

Is there a swimming pool?

Try it out

All the As

Only the letter 'a' remains in these words. Use the definition to fill them in.

1 - a - - - a - - - -
a place to sleep
2 - - - - - - a
… and a way to make sure you get it
3 - - a - -
necessary to get into your room
4 - a - a
sweet dreams on this!
5 - a - a - - - - -
don't lose this – you may have to show it
6 a - - - - - - -
an easy way of getting to the top floor …
7 - - a - - - a
… and another, not quite so easy
8 - - - - a - - a - - -
the place you usually eat in …
9 - - - a - - - -
… the first meal of the day …
10 - - - a
… and the last
11 - - - - a
the place to freshen up …
12 a - - a
… and what comes out of it

Mix-up

The different parts of this conversation have got mixed up. Try to sort them out by putting the letters in the correct order.

A Muchas gracias.
B Sí, aquí a la derecha.
C Sí. ¿Cuánto es?
D Son siete mil setecientas la habitación.
E De nada. Hasta luego.
F No, el desayuno es aparte, a ochocientas pesetas por persona.
G Muy bien. La tomamos.
H Desde las siete de la mañana hasta las diez.
I Gracias. ¿Hay ascensor?
J Sí . . . ¿una habitación doble?
K Ah, y ¿a qué hora es el desayuno?
L Es la habitación número quinientos treinta y cuatro. Aquí tiene la llave.
M Buenas tardes, ¿tienen una habitación libre para una noche?
N ¿Desayuno incluido?

Buying things

El Rastro, Madrid

Prices in Spain are generally comparable to the rest of Europe, and certain electrical goods, toiletries and even food can be expensive.

Larger shops and supermarkets accept major credit cards. Shops are generally open from 9.00 or 10.00 am until 2.00 pm and from 5.00 pm until 8.00 pm on weekdays. Most close at 2.00 pm on Saturday and all day Sunday, though you will normally find somewhere in each *barrio* to buy basics like bread, drinks and snacks. Larger supermarkets, hypermarkets, chain stores and smaller shops in tourist areas stay open all day, often until 10.00 pm. One Spanish institution you will probably not miss is the El Corte Inglés chain, the only department store with centres in every decent-sized town. There you can buy everything from food and jewellery to camping gear, and do everything from booking excursions or seats for a concert or the theatre, to having your hair done. In larger cities you will find names like Marks and Spencer, C&A and The Body Shop.

How can I help you?
¿En qué puedo servirle?

Good value buys

Shoes and leather goods are relatively cheap, and it is easy to find well-made, elegant or original designs. Get bargains around Alicante and in the Balearic islands, Spain's shoe-producing centres.

Ceramics and *azulejos* (floor and wall tiles) The most traditional come from Talavera de la Reina in La Mancha, but they are sold all over Spain. Each locality has its own special designs.

Wine, *cava* and *licores* These are all good value. You can buy most local specialities such as *jerez* (sherry), *cava* (sparkling wine) or *orujo* (a liqueur) all over Spain.

Olive oil is a true delicacy. It can be pricey, but treat yourself to a good bottle for salads. The higher the *acidez* (acidity) (0.7%/0.9%) the stronger, richer and more distinctive the flavour.

Handwoven rugs are colourful and cheap. Try most outdoor markets and craft stores, especially those in Cáceres, Granada or Murcia.

Silver goods are renowned in and around Córdoba, though you can find bargains elsewhere.

Metalwork Knives, swords and sabres crafted in black steel and in-laid with intricate gold leaf are a particular speciality of Toledo. Smaller gifts like earrings and pendants are also available and sold in other parts of Spain; Vigo in Galicia specializes in knives.

Wickerwork This craft is especially developed in Tenerife.

Markets and buying food

Food is generally quite expensive in Spain, but produce is always fresh with a great variety of seafoods, special cured hams, *chorizos* (sausages) and cheeses that are far more expensive in restaurants.

If you are self-catering, your best bet for buying fresh food is the local central market; just about any town has one, or try the *museo del jamón* for hams, sausages and cheeses. Most towns have occasional weekly or monthly clothes or flea markets. Some of the best include:

The Rastro, Madrid, a weekly flea market, ideal for buying cassettes, clothes and souvenirs.

Boquería, Barcelona, a bustling and colourful daily food market, worth a visit for its atmosphere and its excellent fresh produce.

Mercado Central, Valencia, a morning food market in a huge girdered building, said to be one of the largest markets in Europe.

! How much is it?
¿Cuánto es?

Phrasemaker
Phrases you can use anywhere

Do you have any (olive oil / gloves)?	¿Tiene (aceite de oliva/ guantes)?
How much is it?/How much are they?	¿Cuánto es?/Cuánto son?
How much are (the bananas / the plums)?	¿A cuánto están (los plátanos / las ciruelas)?
I'll have (two kilos / a hundred grams), please.	Déme (dos kilos / cien gramos).
This one/That one	Este/Aquél
These/Those	Estos/Aquéllos
How much is it (altogether)?	¿Cuánto es (en total)?
Nothing else, thanks.	Nada más, gracias.
Do you have anything cheaper?	¿Tiene algo más barato?

¿En qué puedo servirle?	Can I help you?
¿Qué desea?	What would you like?
¿Cuánto/Cuánta quiere?	How much would you like?
¿Cuántos/Cuántas quiere?	How many would you like?
¿Algo más?	Anything else?
Lo siento, no tenemos / No, no hay.	I'm sorry, we don't have any.
Aquí tiene.	Here you are.
Son quinientas cuarenta pesetas.	That's five hundred and forty pesetas.

Where to shop

Carnicería	Butcher's
Charcutería	Delicatessen
Comestibles /	Grocer's
Alimentación	
Estanco	Tobacconist's
Panadería /	Baker's,
Pastelería	cake shop
Papelería	Stationer's

Quiosco	Newspaper stand
Relojería /	Watchmaker's /
Joyería	Jeweller's
Supermercado	Supermarket
Verdulería /	Greengrocer's /
Frutería	Fruiterer's
Zapatería	Shoe shop
Mercado	Market

... and when

Things to buy – and where to buy them
The market

apples	**las manzanas**	lemons	**los limones**
apricots	**los albarico-**	lettuce	**la lechuga**
	ques	melon	**el melón**
artichokes	**las alcachofas**	mushrooms	**los champi-**
asparagus	**los espárragos**		**ñones**
aubergines	**las berenjenas**		
avocado	**el aguacate**	onions	**las cebollas**
bananas	**los plátanos**	oranges	**las naranjas**
black grapes	**las uvas negras**	peaches	**los meloco-**
cauliflower	**la coliflor**		**tones**
celery	**el apio**	pears	**las peras**
cherries	**las cerezas**	pepper	**el pimiento**
chickpeas	**los garbanzos**	pineapple	**la piña**
cucumber	**el pepino**	plums	**las ciruelas**
fig	**el higo**	potatoes	**las patatas**
green grapes	**las uvas verdes**	strawberries	**las fresas**
leek	**el puerro**	tomatoes	**los tomates**
		water-melon	**la sandía**

61

Grocer's shop, food store

(a loaf of) bread	**(una barra de) pan**	cheese	**el queso**
(orange / apple) juice	**el zumo de (naranja / manzana)**	coffee	**el café**
(red / white) wine	**el vino (tinto / blanco)**	cured ham	**el jamón serrano**
anchovies	**las anchoas**	eggs	**los huevos**
beer	**la cerveza**	milk	**la leche**
boiled ham	**el jamón de York**	olive oil	**el aceite de oliva**
butter	**la mantequilla**	sardines	**las sardinas**
cake	**el pastel**	sausage	**el chorizo, el salchichón**
		tea	**el té**
		yoghurt	**el yogur**

Weights, measures and containers

cien gramos	100g
doscientos cincuenta gramos	250g
medio kilo	½k
una lata	a tin
un cuarto de kilo	¼k
un kilo	1k
un litro	1 litre
un paquete	a packet
una barra de pan	loaf of bread
una bolsa	a bag
una botella	a bottle
una docena	dozen

Men's / women's fashionwear

belt	**un cinturón**	socks	**los calcetines**
blouse	**una blusa**	stockings / tights	**unas medias**
boots	**las botas**		
coat	**un abrigo**	sweater	**un suéter / un jersey**
dress	**un vestido**		
hat	**un sombrero**	swimming costume	**un bañador**
jacket	**una chaqueta**		
jeans	**los vaqueros**	tie	**una corbata**
knickers	**una braga**	trousers	**un pantalón**
scarf	**una bufanda**	underpants	**un calzoncillo**
shirt	**una camisa**	vest	**una camiseta**

Material

A leather shirt	**Una camisa de cuero / de piel**
A (wool / cotton / polyester) sweater	**Un suéter de (lana / algodón / poliéster)**

Newspaper stand / stationer's / tobacconist's

cigarettes	**los cigarrillos**	magazines	**las revistas**
cigars	**los puros**	newspaper stand	**el quiosco**
a guide	**una guía**		
a map	**un mapa**	postcards	**las postales**
a plan	**un plano**	stationer's	**la papelería**
a stamp	**un sello**	stationer's / tobacconist's	**el estanco**
foreign papers	**los periódicos extranjeros**	tobacco	**el tabaco**

Souvenirs and gifts

bracelet	**una pulsera**	ring	**un anillo**
cassette	**una cassette**	t-shirt	**una camiseta**
CD-ROM	**un CD-ROM**	toy	**un juguete**
necklace	**un collar**	watch	**un reloj**
purse	**un monedero**	earrings	**unos pendientes**

Shopping in a store

Sótano	Basement
Planta baja	ground floor
Planta primera	1st floor
Planta segunda	2nd floor
Planta tercera	3rd floor
Planta cuarta	4th floor

Alimentación	Food
Juguetes	Toys
Moda de señoras	Ladies' fashion
Moda de caballeros	Men's fashion
Ferretería	Hardware

Where is the music department?	¿Dónde está la sección de música?
What floor is it on?	¿En qué planta está?
Is there a lift?	¿Hay ascensor?
Está en la planta baja.	It's on the ground floor.

Trying on and buying clothes

I'd like (a skirt / a tie).	Quisiera (una falda / una corbata).
Do you have the same in green?	¿Tiene lo mismo en verde?
Can I try it on?	¿Puedo probármelo/la?*
Can I try them on?	¿Puedo probármelos/las?*
It's a bit big.	Es un poco grande.
It's a bit small.	Es un poco pequeño/a.*
They're a bit big.	Son un poco grandes.
They're a bit small.	Son un poco pequeños/as.*
Have you got anything (bigger / smaller / cheaper)?	¿Tiene algo más (grande / pequeño/a / barato/a)?
How much (is it/are they)?	¿Cuánto (es/son)?
I like it/I like them.	Me gusta/Me gustan.
I'll take it.	Me lo/la llevo.
I'll take them.	Me los/las llevo.
Do you take credit cards?	¿Aceptan tarjetas de crédito?
¿Qué talla? / ¿Qué número?	What size?
Claro.	Of course.
Por aquí.	This way.
Le queda bien.	It suits you.

(*If you want to be really accurate, check in Language builder p108)

Buying stamps

How much is a stamp for Europe?
¿Cuánto vale un sello para Europa?

Two sixty-peseta stamps, please.
Déme dos sellos de sesenta pesetas.

Buying foreign newspapers

Do you have any (English) newspapers?
¿Tiene periódicos (ingleses)?

Do you have any magazines in (French / Italian)?
¿Tiene revistas en (francés / italiano)?

Sólo tengo . . . I only have . . .
No tengo . . . I don't have . . .

Buying and developing films

colour film **una película en color**
black and white film **una película en blanco y negro**
battery **una pila**
Will you develop this film, please? **¿Me revela este carrete?**
When will it be ready? **¿Cuándo estará listo?**

Mañana por la (mañana / tarde) Tomorrow (morning / afternoon)
En (una hora / veinticuatro horas) In (one hour / 24 hours)

At the grocer's

3 You prepare for a picnic
- Buenos días.
- □ Buenos días, una barra de pan, y ¿tiene jamón de York?
- No, sólo hay jamón serrano.
- □ Déme doscientos gramos, y medio kilo de queso.
- Muy bien, ¿algo más?
- □ Sí, una botella de zumo de piña . . . ¿Cuánto es?
- Setecientas noventa el jamón, quinientas veinte el queso, y el zumo . . . son mil cuatrocientas veinte en total.
- □ Aquí tiene . . . adiós.
- Adiós, gracias.

Which was the most expensive item? And which the least?

Buying stamps

4 You're ready to send cards home
- ¿Cuánto vale un sello para Europa?
- □ Son sesenta pesetas.
- Déme tres sellos de sesenta pesetas.

How much did you pay?

| **Language works** |

Shopping at the market

1 You buy the fruit you want – almost!
- ¿Qué desea?
- □ ¿Tiene melocotones?
- No, no hay.
- □ ¿A cuánto están los albaricoques?
- A cuatrocientas diez pesetas el kilo.
- □ Déme dos kilos de albaricoques, y una sandía.
- Muy bien . . . ¿Algo más?
- □ No, gracias. ¿Cuánto es?
- Son novecientas ochenta pesetas en total.

How much was the watermelon?

Buying clothes

2 You get the trousers you deserve
- Buenas tardes. Quisiera un pantalón.
- □ ¿De poliéster?
- No, de algodón. Talla dieciséis.
- □ ¿Le gusta éste?
- Sí, pero ¿tiene el mismo en azul?
- □ Sí.
- ¿Puedo probármelo?
- □ Claro, por aquí . . . . . . Le queda muy bien.
- Sí, ¿cuánto es?
- □ Siete mil trescientas pesetas.
- Muy bien, me lo llevo.

What did the assistant think of your trousers?

Having a film developed

5 You ask about your holiday prints

- ¿Me revela este carrete?
- □ Claro.
- ¿Cuándo estará listo?
- □ Mañana por la tarde.
- Muy bien.

When will your film be ready?

Sound Check

r
r at the beginning of a word, and **rr** are strongly rolled, like the **r** in Scottish 'bairn'.

revista	rayveesta
barra	bara

In between vowels / in the middle of a word, **r** is still rolled but not as strongly:

caro	caroh

Practise with these words:
reloj, carrete, cereza

Try it out

Syllable salad

Rearrange the syllables in these words to make things you can eat or drink.

mozu	tanoplá
mónja	tóncomelo
chocaalfa	soque
vohue	nadisar
janaran	zarece

Mix and match

Match each of the phrases 1 – 8 with the best reply a – h.
1. ¿En qué puedo servirle?
2. ¿Algo más?
3. ¿Qué número?
4. ¿Cuánto quiere?
5. ¿Cuánto es?
6. ¿A cuánto están las naranjas?

a El catorce
b A ciento noventa pesetas el kilo
c Deme quinientos gramos
d ¿Tiene CD-ROM?
e Mil doscientas veinticinco pesetas
f No, nada más, gracias

As if you were there

You go into a grocer's shop one morning to buy things for a picnic.
- (Greet the shopkeeper)
- □ Buenos días, ¿qué desea?
- (Ask for two hundred grams of cured ham)
- □ Muy bien. ¿Algo más?
- (Ask if they have any bread)
- □ Sí. ¿Barra pequeña o grande?
- (a large loaf)
- □ ¿Algo más?
- (Say that's all, thanks, and ask how much)
- □ Mil trescientas pesetas.
- (Hand over the money . . . thank her and say good-bye)

Café life

Café Gijón, Madrid

Meal times

The Spanish love eating and drinking out throughout the year.
In the evenings and at weekends, families frequently go out en masse for a communal meal since a three-course *menú del día* (set lunch or dinner) can be had at a very reason-able price.

At breakfast, cafés are busy from 7.00 am until 9.00 am with people taking a strong coffee and a *bollo* (roll) or *una pasta* (pastry). It is worth remembering that restaurants have relatively strict opening hours, and it is almost impossible to find one that will serve you outside these times, which are usually from around 1.30 pm until 4.00 pm and from 8.00 pm until 12.00 or 12.30 am. At lunchtime, bars and cafés (which have longer opening hours) and restaurants are filled with workers who do not have time to go home for the traditional midday meal and *siesta*, especially from 2.00 until 4.00 pm. From 6.00 until 8.00 pm, these places fill up again when people stop for the *merienda* (an afternoon snack) to keep them going until dinner which can be any time between 9.00 and 10.00 pm.

What tapas do you have?
¿Qué tapas tienen?

Where to eat

Spain has the most bars, cafés and restaurants per head of population in Europe, so you are sure to find something to suit your taste.
Cafeterías are your surest bet for breakfast and afternoon tea. Even the most basic offer good coffee, tea and a range of freshly-baked pastries and croissants. Cafés are also good for a light lunch of *bocadillos* (long

bread rolls stuffed with savoury fillings) and *montados* (a half-sized version) or a *sandwich mixto*, a toasted sandwich with cheese and ham. Wherever you go, you will also find a dazzling choice of hot and cold *tapas* (snacks) and *raciones* (bigger helpings of the same). Some cafés may offer more substantial midday meals. *Platos combinados* are set dishes, where a selection of food, such as *tortilla española* or *jamón serrano* is served on one plate. They can be good value. The *menú del día* usually consists of a choice from a set menu of three or more starters, main courses and desserts or coffee and includes bread, wine, beer or a soft drink.

Tascas are small and often very old bars full of character, where *tapas* and *raciones* are also served. They are usually tucked away in the narrow streets of the older parts of town.

Bodegas are old, traditional bars selling wine, sherry and beer to drink in or take away. They usually have a wide selection of *tapas* and *raciones* on offer.

Cervecerías, tabernas and mesones are usually larger and have a greater if more expensive array of dishes. Many specialize in food from different regions of Spain.

Restaurantes are the best places to have a tranquil sit-down meal. Generally restaurants are classified from two to five forks, with five forks signifying luxury and prices to match. However, many restaurants have no formal classification, yet serve wonderful typically Spanish food at incredibly reasonable prices. Do not always be put off if you think prices seem cheap; you may have come across a gem. All but the most exclusive restaurants have a *menú del día* or *menú especial*, but you can also eat as little or as much as you like by choosing individual items from the menu, *tapas* style. The à la carte selections tend to offer special regional dishes, as well as certain international dishes.

Marisquerías serve a tempting array of dishes prepared with ingredients fresh from the sea, even in cities far from the coast, and quality is generally guaranteed, though meals can be expensive.

Fast-food places are taking off in Spain, which is now peppered with burger and hot-dog bars, pizza places and *Bocadillerías* serving *bocadillos* with chips and a soft drink or beer.

I'd like a portion of prawns.
¡Póngame una ración de gambas!

Phrasemaker

Asking what they have

Do you have (ice-cream / sandwiches)?	**¿Tienen (helados / bocadillos)?**
Do you have any tapas (snacks)?	**¿Hay tapas?**
What tapas do you have?	**¿Qué tapas tienen?**
What cool drinks do you have?	**¿Qué refrescos tienen?**

Ordering

I'll have a portion of omelette.	**Póngame una ración de tortilla.**
We'll have a portion of ham and some mushrooms.	**Pónganos una ración de jamón y unos champiñones.**
A vanilla ice-cream, please.	**Un helada de Vainilla, por favor**
A glass of white wine for me.	**Para mí, un vaso de vino blanco.**
This one/That one	**Este/Aquél**

Paying

How much is it?	**¿Cuánto es?**
Here you are	**Tenga. / Aquí tiene.**

¿Qué desea/n?	What would you like?
¿Quiere alguna tapa?	Would you like a tapa?
Lo siento, no hay.	Sorry, we don't have any.
En seguida	Right away

Cool drinks

cold chocolate	**un chocolate frío**
cool drinks	**refrescos**
drinks	**bebidas**
fizzy (orange / lemon) drink	**una (naranjada / limonada)**
glass of milk	**un vaso de leche**
iced coffee	**un café con hielo**
iced (lemon / melon) drink	**un granizado de (limón / melón)**
lemonade	**una gaseosa**
milky nut-based drink	**una horchata**
(orange / tomato / pineapple / apple / grapefruit) juice	**un zumo de (naranja / tomate / piña / manzana / pomelo)**
(sparkling / still) mineral water	**una agua mineral (con gas / sin gas)**
tea	**un té**
tonic water	**una tónica**

Hot drinks

(black / slightly white / creamy / decaffeinated) coffee	**un café (solo / cortado / con leche / descafeinado)**
camomile tea	**una manzanilla**
herbal tea	**una infusión**
hot chocolate	**un chocolate**
hot drinks	**bebidas calientes**
Irish coffee	**un café irlandés**
mint tea	**un poleo**

Alcoholic drinks

alcoholic drinks	**bebidas alcohólicas**
anis(ette)	**un anís**
aperitif	**un aperitivo**
beer (bottled)	**una cerveza**
bottle of Spanish sparkling wine	**una botella de cava**
brandy	**un coñac**
cider	**una sidra**
cubalibre (coke and white rum)	**un cubalibre**
dry sherry	**un fino**
glass of brandy	**una copa de coñac**
glass of draught beer	**una caña**
glass of (dry / sweet / semi-sweet) white wine	**un vaso de vino blanco (seco / dulce / semi-seco)**
gin	**una ginebra**
gin and tonic	**un gintonic**
red / rosé wine	**un vino tinto / rosado**
rum	**un ron**
sangría (red wine and fruit juice)	**una sangría**
shandy	**una clara**
sherry	**un jerez**
small draught beer	**una media caña**
vermouth	**un vermút**

Ice-creams

chocolate	**chocolate**
coffee	**café**
flavours	**sabores**
ice-cream parlour / shop	**una heladería**
ice-creams	**helados**
raspberry	**frambuesa**
strawberry	**fresa**
vanilla	**vainilla**
wafer / cornet	**un (barquillo / cornete)**

Tapas

These are the snacks worth going to Spain for. Tapas can be almost anything – look for local specialities. Here are some of the more common ones:

ensaladilla Rusa

calamares a la romana

aceitunas	olives
anchoas	anchovies (brown)
atún	tuna
boquerones	anchovies (silver)
calamares a la romana	fried squid
calamares en su tinta	squid in its ink
caracoles de (tierra / mar)	snails / whelks
champiñones	mushrooms
empanadilla	small (meat / fish)
de (carne / pescado)	pasty
ensaladilla rusa	Russian salad
gambas a la plancha	grilled prawns
lomo de cerdo	pork loin (pieces)
mejillones	mussels
patatas fritas	crisps, chips
pulpo	octopus
queso (manchego)	cheese
	(from La Mancha)
sardinas	sardines
sepia	cuttlefish
tortilla española / tortilla	Spanish omelette
de patata	

BAR CAFETERÍA
MI TATE
Especialidad en desayunos
Tostadas con pan de Las Cabezas y la rica semilla de Sanlucar

Sandwiches and pastry mixes

round fritters	**buñuelos**
sweet buns	**chuchos (Xuxos)**
fritters	**churros**
sandwich	**un bocadillo**
toasted sandwich	**un sandwich**

Cakes

bun	**una madalena**
cake	**un pastel**
nougat	**el turrón**
sponge biscuit	**un bizcocho**
tart, pie	**una tarta**

Containers

carafe	**una garrafa**
cup	**una taza**
pitcher	**una jarra**
sherry glass	**una copita**
tumbler	**un vaso**
wine glass	**una copa**

Signs to look for

toilets	**Servicios**
washroom	**Lavabos**
bathroom	**Baño**
Ladies	**Señoras**
Gentlemen	**Caballeros**

Sound Check

ch
ch in Spanish is pronounced like the English 'ch' in 'church', wherever it occurs in a word.

chocolate	chokolateh
anchoas	anchoas

Practise with these words:
champiñones, horchata, churros, leche, bizcocho

Language works

Ordering drinks

1 Cooling down with a friend
- **Buenas tardes ¿Qué desean?**
- □ **Buenas tardes. ¿Qué refrescos tienen?**
- **Tenemos zumo de piña y de naranja, granizado de limón y horchata . . .**
- □ **Pónganos un granizado de limón y una cerveza.**
- **Muy bien.**

You were offered three juice drinks and one creamy one: true/false?
What drinks did you decide against?

A taste of the tapas

2 You and your partner have a difficult choice
- **Buenas tardes. ¿Qué tapas tienen?**
- □ **Pues, hay calamares, gambas, tortilla española, queso, ensaladilla rusa . . .**
- **Pónganos una ración de gambas y una de tortilla y . . . ¿hay patatas fritas?**
- □ **¡Claro! ¿Dos raciones?**
- **Sí, gracias . . . y un fino y un vino tinto.**
- □ **En seguida . . .**
- **¿Cuánto es?**

- □ **Son ochocientas veinte pesetas.**
- **Tenga.**

Which seafood tapas could you have had?
How much did you pay?

Sandwiches for lunch

3 A range of choice
- **Buenas tardes. ¿Hay bocadillos?**
- □ **Sí, hay bocadillos de jamón, queso, chorizo, atún.**
- **¿Tiene tortilla?**
- □ **Sí, hay bocadillos de tortilla española.**
- **Pues, un bocadillo de jamón y uno de tortilla española.**
- □ **En seguida.**

What kind of sandwich does the waiter offer you?

Coffee in the open air

4 You order coffee for a group of four
- **Buenas tardes, ¿Qué desean?**
- □ **Cuatro cafés.**
- **¿Solos?**
- □ **No, un solo y tres cortados.**
- **¿Coñac?**
- □ **Sí, cuatro.**
- **Muy bien.**

What do you all have as well as coffee?

Try it out

Mixing them

Take one word from the left column and, if necessary, add **de** and a word from the right column. (Three of the words from the left will stand alone)

Una copa	
Un vaso	calamares
Una botella	coñac
Una media caña de	té
Una caña	cava
Una ración	fresa
Una taza	tinto
Un fino	

Allergies

Look at this *tapas* menu, and pick out those that would not be suitable for a friend who was allergic to a) fish, b) eggs and dairy produce and c) meat.
What could they choose?

Gambas a la plancha	Sardinas
Anchoas	Chorizo
Boquerones	Tortilla española
Queso manchego	Aceitunas
Mejillones	Caracoles de mar
Ensaladilla rusa	
Empanadillas de carne	

Split the difference

Combine these halves of words, then find the one that is not a drink.

zu	nebra
gas	lado
ca	gría
cer	nizado
he	eosa
ca	cafeinado
des	va
gra	mo
san	fé
gi	veza

As if you were there

An evening in the Plaza Mayor of Trujillo. You savour the atmosphere and the café life with two friends. As you sit on the terraza of a café, a waiter approaches.

- **Buenas tardes, ¿qué desean?**
- □ (Greet him, and order a beer, a vermouth and a white wine)
- **Muy bien. ¿Quieren alguna tapa?**
- □ (Ask what they have)
- **Pues, tenemos chorizo, jamón serrano, tortilla, boquerones, patatas ali-oli, lomo de cerdo.**
- □ (Ask for a portion of ham, anchovies and omelette)
- **Muy bien . . .**
- □ (When you have finished, you call the waiter, and ask him how much it is)
- **Son mil seiscientas treinta pesetas.**

Eating out

Courses

So the Spanish diet is one of the healthiest and most well-balanced in Europe. Fresh salads, vegetables and fruits figure highly in every menu though there is a tendency to fry vegetables in olive oil and garlic. The Spanish eat as much fish and seafood as they do meat and poultry, served plain or with a local sauce. At a sit-down meal, you can choose from:

■ **Entradas / Primer Plato** A selection of salads, vegetables, cold meats, hot or cold soups or fish.
■ **Segundo Plato** Meat, fish, seafood, *tortilla* or *revuelto* (scrambled egg dishes with other ingredients) and a small garnish.
■ **Postres,** often home-made puddings or cakes, ice-cream, custard tart, rice pudding or a piece of fruit. Do not forget the *copita* with your coffee, a shot or small glass of liqueur, brandy or whisky.

Vegetarian options can be limited; even vegetable dishes are often made with meat stock or contain pieces of meat. Omelettes and salads are guaranteed fall-backs.

❗ A table for two.
Una mesa para do

Ten Spanish dishes not to be missed

Tortilla española, a filling potato omelette.
Patatas ali-oli, Catalan potato snack prepared with garlic and olive oil.
Gazpacho, a chilled Andalusian soup made with fresh tomatoes, cucumber, onion, garlic and olive oil.
Jamón serrano, succulent cured ham.
Queso curado, strong mature cheese usually made from goat's milk.
Chorizo ibérico, a kind of sausage spiced with paprika.
Boquerones en vinagre, tiny white baby anchovy fillets prepared with garlic and fresh parsley.
Pincho moruno, marinated pork kebabs.
Pulpo gallego, Galician octopus prepared on a griddle with special seasoning.
Paella, a Valencian rice dish made with fresh seafood, or a mixture of fish, seafood and pork, chicken or rabbit.

Regional specialities

The North is the area for sauces, the Pyrenees is famed for its *chilindrones* (tomato and pepper accompaniments), Cataluña for its *cazuelas* (stews) and the East coast for its rice dishes. In Andalusia go for the fried dishes and on the central plain for roasts.

Is there a set menu?
¿Hay menú del día?

If you are in the area or in a regional restaurant try the following:
Galicia *Mariscos* (all seafood in general is excellent); *Empanada* (fish and seafood pasty); *Queso de tetilla* (a creamy plain or smoked cow's cheese).
Asturias *Fabada* (white bean stew with *morcilla* – black pudding – cured hams and bacon). *Merluza a la sidra* (hake cooked in the local cider). *Queso cabrales* (extremely strong blue cheese).
El país vasco *Bacalao a la vizcaína* (cod cooked with peppers and onions); *angulas* (baby eels dipped in boiling olive oil with garlic and hot red pepper); *idiazabal* (strong goat's cheese with a smoky flavour).

Aragón *Pollo al chilindrón* (chicken with tomato and pepper); *Las magras con tomate* (slices of ham delicately fried and dipped in tomato sauce); *Longaniza* (spicy sausage).

Barcelona *Fideos a la cazuela* (soup with noodles, spare ribs, sausage and bacon); *Crema Catalana* (custard covered with caramel).
Valencia *Arroz empedrado* (rice with tomatoes, cod and a layer of white beans); *La collá* (a yoghurt made with wild artichokes).
Andalusia *Jamón de Jabugo* (exquisite cured ham from Huelva); *Pescaíto frito* (deep-fried *boquerones*); *Pescado en adobo* (fish in spicy batter).
Castilla-León *Cochinillo* (whole roast suckling pig); *Cordero asado* (roast lamb).
Extremadura *Jamón de Bellota* (cured ham from acorn-fed pigs).
La Mancha *Pisto Manchego* (tasty stew made from fresh tomatoes, peppers, garlic and egg); *Zorajo* (tripe with a spicy sauce).
Madrid *Cocido Madrileño* (a hearty soup made with meat, pulses and vegetables, served in three courses, *vuelcos*).
Islas Canarias *Viejas con papas arrugadas* (parrot fish and potato dish with *mojo* sauce); *El gofio* (bread from

an ancient recipe made with wheat, maize or chick-pea flour). Bananas feature in many dishes.

Islas Baleares *El Tumbet* (potato and aubergine cake covered in tomato sauce and peppers); *La caldereta de langosta* (lobster stewed with peppers, onion, garlic, tomatoes and herb liqueur); *Ensaimada* (delicate puff pastry dusted with sugar).

Wines, drinks and spirits you must try:

A bottle of red wine
Una botella de vino tinto

Wines Quality *Denominación de Origen* wines include Rioja and the young, light La Mancha and Valdepeñas; the pale dry Rueda or Ribeira del Duero; and Albariño, a dry Galician white. Penedés are light wines while Priorato is a dark, heavy red with a velvety flavour. Campo de Borja and Somontano are heavy reds from Aragón; Navarra is excellent for reds, whites and rosés; while young Jumilla wines from Murcia, strong Alicante reds and rosés, and Valencia dry whites are also recommended.

Cava A delicious inexpensive Spanish sparkling wine from Cataluña.

Jerez (sherry) Of the ten main groups of sherries, try the dry, light *Fino*; the amber medium *Amontillado*; the dark golden *Oloroso* and the sweet *Moscatel*.

Pacharán A raisin-based liqueur from Navarra.

Anís A strong dry or sweet alcoholic drink made from aniseed.

Orujo A strong Galician drink distilled from the grapes left over from wine-making. Try it in *La queimada*, made by burning the *orujo* in an earthenware pot with lemon, sugar and coffee beans.

Sangría A potent punch made with red wine, fruit juice and spirits.

Tinto de verano A refreshing mix of red wine and *gaseosa* (lemonade) with a dash of lemon juice.

Limón granizado A zesty summer drink made with fresh lemon juice, sugar and ground ice.

Horchata An unusual milky drink made from tiger nuts.

Coffees Try *café con leche* (milky coffee, the usual order for breakfast); *café solo* (strong black coffee); *café cortado* (a strong black coffee with a tiny dash of milk); *café con hielo* (strong black coffee served on ice as a reviving summer drink); or *carajillo* (strong black coffee with a large dash of whisky, brandy, or rum, an ideal winter warmer).

Four white coffees, please.
Cuatro cafés con leche.

Phrasemaker
Finding somewhere to eat

Is there a good restaurant near here?

¿**Hay un buen restaurante por aquí?**

At the restaurant

ashtray	**el cenicero**
bottle	**la botella**
chair	**la silla**
fork	**el tenedor**
glass	**el vaso**
knife	**el cuchillo**
napkin	**la servilleta**
oil	**el aceite**
pepper	**la pimienta**
plate	**el plato**
salt	**la sal**
saucer	**el platillo**
spoon	**la cuchara**
table	**la mesa**
tablecloth	**el mantel**
teaspoon	**la cucharilla**
toothpick	**el palillo de dientes**
vinegar	**el vinagre**

Arriving

A table for (two / four).
We have a reservation for three.

Una mesa para (dos / cuatro).
Tenemos una reserva para tres.

Por aquí   This way

Asking about the menu

The menu, please.	**La carta, por favor.**
Is there a set menu?	**¿Hay menú del día?**
What's the set menu?	**¿Cuál es el menú del día?**
Do you have any (crab / chicken)?	**¿Tienen (cangrejo / pollo)?**
What is (besugo al horno / merluza a la vizcaína)?	**¿Qué es (besugo al horno / merluza a la vizcaína)?**
What are (callos a la madrileña / natillas)?	**¿Qué son (callos a la madrileña / natillas)?**
What is (gazpacho / paella) like?	**¿Cómo es (el gazpacho / la paella)?**
What are (huevos a la flamenca) like?	**¿Cómo son (los huevos a la flamenca)?**
What's the local speciality?	**¿Cuál es el plato típico de aquí?**

Ordering

A garlic soup for me.	**Para mí, una sopa de ajo.**
A squid	**Una de calamares**
What would you like for (first course / starters / second course / main course / dessert)?	**¿Qué van a tomar de (primer plato / primero / segundo / plato principal / postre)?**
Could we have . . .	**Tráiganos . . .**
(a bottle / half a bottle / a glass) of (red / white / rosé) wine	**(una botella / media botella / un vaso) de vino (tinto / blanco / rosado)**
two beers	**dos cervezas**
(sparkling / still) mineral water	**agua mineral (con gas / sin gas)**
a dry sherry	**un fino**

¿Qué desean?	What would you like?
¿Van a tomar postre?	Are you going to have any dessert?
¿Quieren beber algo?	Would you like anything to drink?
¿Qué van a beber?	What would you like to drink?
¿Y para beber?	Anything to drink?
El menú del día es . . .	Today's special menu is . . .
Hoy tenemos . . .	Today we have . . .
Lo siento, no hay . . .	Sorry, we don't have any . . .
¿Cómo lo quieren?	How would you like it?
Es un pescado blanco.	It's a white fish.
Es una especie de tarta.	It's a sort of tart.
Muy bien	Fine

Eating preferences

I'm vegetarian.	**Soy vegetariano/a.**
I don't eat (meat / fish / seafood).	**No como (carne / pescado / mariscos).**
Does it contain (salt / sugar / chilli / nuts)?	**¿Tiene (sal / azúcar / chile / nueces)?**

During the meal

Excuse me!	**¡Oiga!**
More (bread / wine), please.	**Más (pan / vino), por favor.**
They're very good.	**Están muy buenos/buenas.** *
It's very good.	**Está muy bueno/buena.** *
It's delicious.	**Está muy rico/rica.** *
It's cold.	**Está frío/a.** *
It's very hot (spicy).	**Es muy picante.**
It's raw.	**Está crudo/a.** *

(*To use these accurately, check Language builder, p108)

¿Todo bien?	Everything OK?
¿Qué tal (la merluza / el besugo)?	What's (the hake / the bream) like?
¿Qué tal (los calamares / las croquetas)?	What are (the squid / the croquettes) like?
¿Algo más?	Anything else?

Paying

The bill, please.	**La cuenta, por favor.**
Is service included?	**¿Está incluido el servicio?**
Do you take credit cards?	**¿Aceptan tarjetas de crédito?**
There's a mistake, I think.	**Hay un error, creo.**
We didn't have this.	**No tomamos esto.**

And . . .

Where are the toilets?	**¿Dónde están los servicios?**

Language works

Arriving

1 You find a table and make a start
- Buenas tardes. ¿Una mesa para dos?
□ Sí, para dos.
- Por aquí. ¿Quieren beber algo?
□ Sí, un fino y un vermút.

Choose: The waiter offers you a snack / a drink / a nice table.

Talking about the menu

2 You have to change your order slightly
- ¿Qué van a tomar?
□ ¿Qué es ensalada 'El Chato'?
- Es la ensalada de la casa. Es muy buena.
□ Bueno, de primero una sopa de pescado y una ensalada.
- Y ¿de segundo?
□ Un besugo al horno y un solomillo.
- Lo siento, hoy no hay besugo.
□ Entonces una chuleta de cerdo.
- ¿Y para beber?
□ Una botella de vino blanco y una botella de agua mineral con gas.
(**Entonces** = then)

Which item is off the menu today?

Ordering drinks

3 You choose wine and water
- ¿Y para beber?
□ Una botella de vino blanco y una botella de agua mineral.
- ¿Con gas?
□ No, una botella grande sin gas.
- Muy bien.

What kind of water does the waiter expect you to have?

Paying

4 You settle amicably
- ¡Camarero! La cuenta, por favor.
□ En seguida . . . Aquí tiene.
- ¿Aceptan tarjetas de crédito?
□ Sí, Visa y Mastercard.
- Muy bien.

How many cards can you pay with?

And finally . . .

5 You start to leave
- ¿Qué tal la cena?
□ Muy buena, muy rica. Por favor, ¿dónde están los servicios?
- Allí.
□ Gracias.
- De nada.

What does the waiter ask you?

Sound Check

j
j in Spanish is pronounced like the 'ch' in the Scottish pronunciation of 'loch'.

cangrejo	kangreyhho
ajo	ahho

Practise with these words:
almeja, mejillones, jerez, lentejas, jabalí

Try it out

Sopa de letras

('Word soup' is what the Spaniards call a wordsearch)

C	S	B	C	J	A	B	A	L	I
E	E	S	O	C	S	I	R	A	M
R	R	A	C	E	R	D	O	J	A
V	A	O	A	L	A	C	A	B	D
E	M	P	P	L	A	T	O	J	A
Z	A	L	O	A	T	N	E	U	L
A	L	U	S	T	R	R	I	C	A
P	A	P	T	G	A	M	B	A	S
O	C	D	R	I	C	O	E	S	N
S	E	S	E	M	E	R	T	N	E

Find the word for:

hors d'œuvres	prawns
seafood	dessert
salad	garlic
squid	soup
beer	cod
octopus	pork
wild boar	

And the words that fit in here:
- ¿Qué tal la merluza?
- ¡Muy ..... !
- ¿Y el bacalao?
- ¡Muy .....!
- ¿Qué van a tomar de primer .....?

Menu-making

Some of these dishes have been placed in the wrong category on the menu. Try to sort them out. (Some of the first and main courses are interchangeable.)

Primer plato
Flan
Gambas a la plancha
Membrillo
Besugo al horno
Riñones al jerez

Plato principal
Crema de espárragos
Jamón serrano
Helados mixtos
Pimientos rellenos
Perdiz 'El Bosque'

Postre
Ensalada de atún
Arroz a la cubana
Solomillo
Champiñones al ajo

As if you were there

You go with your partner one evening to a nice fish restaurant in Santander, on the north coast.
- (Greet the waiter and say you'd like a table for two)
- □ **Muy bien . . . ¿Quieren beber algo?**
- (Ask for a glass of red wine and a sherry)

The waiter comes back after you've looked at the menu
- □ **¿Qué van a tomar?**
- (Ask what the '*Langostas a la santanderina*' are like)
- □ **Son muy buenas, a la plancha con un poco de ajo, pero poco.**
- (Sounds OK! Order two of them, and an onion soup and a salad)

The waiter comes up again.
- □ **¿Qué tal la langosta?**
- (Great!)
- □ **¿Van a tomar postre?**
- (You're full. Ask for the bill)

Menu reader

Menus

menú del día
fixed-price menu
pan y cubierto
bread and cover charge
pan y vino incluidos
bread and wine included
propina
tip
servicio (no) incluido
service (not) included
plato del día
dish of the day
platos combinados
set dishes

What to expect

These are the main categories of dish you will be offered on the menu (*la carta*).

Entradas / Primer plato
Starters

Starters usually include a selection of salads, vegetables, cold meats, hot or cold soups or fish. Look out for *el gazpacho*, a cold, spicy tomato soup with cucumber, onion and croutons and *calamares a la romana*, rings of squid deep fried in batter. Eat them hot. *Jamón serrano* is also a popular starter dish, the dry, cured ham is delicious with some bread and a sprinkling of oil.

jamón serrano

Plato principal / Segundo plato
Main course

Meat (*carne*), fish (*pescado*), seafood (*mariscos*), egg dishes (*tortilla / revuelto*), chicken dishes (*pollo*) served with a side-salad (*ensalada*), chips / potato croquettes (*patatas fritas / croquetas*) or vegetables (*verduras*). Meat dishes include *chuletas de cerdo* and *rosbif* with *besugo al horno* (baked sea bream) as a good fish dish. *Pollo al ajillo* (garlic chicken) is a very popular chicken dish.

Postres
Desserts

membrillo

This is usually a home-made pudding or cake, ice-cream, custard tart, rice pudding or a piece of fruit. *Membrillo* (quince jelly) is a popular dessert often served with soft cheese, while *flan* (crème caramel) is always available.

Main ways of cooking

a la plancha / a la parrilla griddled / grilled
a la romana deep-fried / in batter
adobo / al adobo pickled / marinated
ahumado/a smoked
al horno in the oven / baked
asado con espetón on the spit
asado/a roast
brasa / a la brasa barbecued
cacerola / en cacerola casseroled
catalán / a la catalana Catalan-style, with onion, tomato and herbs
cazuela / a la cazuela casseroled
cocido al vapor steamed
cocido/a boiled / stewed
crudo raw
empanado/a breaded and fried
en su tinta in its ink
escabechado/a / en escabeche pickled / soused / marinated
estofado stewed
fresco/a fresh
frío/a cold
frito/a fried
guisado/a stewed
gusto / a su gusto to your choice
hervido/a boiled

horno / al horno baked
natural / al natural fresh / raw
país / del país local
parrilla / a la parilla barbecued / grilled
picado minced
plancha / a la plancha grilled (on a griddle)
rebozado/a battered / breaded and fried
rehogado/a sautéed
relleno/a stuffed
romano / a la romana deep-fried in batter
salteado/a sautéed
vapor / al vapor steamed
vinagre / en vinagre pickled
poco hecho/a underdone / rare
a punto medium
bien hecho/a well done

cacerola de tomates y pimientos

The menu

aceite oil
aceitunas olives
aguacate avocado
ajo garlic
albóndigas meatballs
alcachofas artichokes
almejas clams
almendras almonds
alubias beans
　blancas butter beans
　pintas red kidney beans
anchoas anchovies
apio celery
arenque herring
arroz rice
　a la cubana rice with a tomato

　　sauce and fried egg
　con leche rice pudding
atún tuna
avellana hazelnut
aves poultry
bacalao cod
　a la vizcaína basque-style cod with peppers, ham, onions, garlic and chilli pepper
berberechos cockles
berenjena aubergine
berza cabbage
besugo sea bream
bistec grilled steak
bonito tuna

boquerones anchovies
brocheta skewer / kebab
brócoli broccoli
buey / de buey beef
butifarra a type of white sausage from Cataluña
caballa mackerel
cabrito kid
cacahuetes peanuts
calabacín courgette
calabaza marrow
calamares squid
caldereta stew
caldo clear soup
caldo gallego clear soup with vegetables, beans and pork
callos tripe
  a la madrileña Madrid-style tripe, in a spicy sausage and tomato sauce
camarones baby prawns
cangrejo crab
caracoles snails
carne meat
castaña chestnut
caza game
cebolla onion
cerdo pork
champiñones mushrooms
chipirones baby squid
chirimoya custard apple
chocolate chocolate
chorizo spicy sausage
chuleta de ternera veal cutlet
cigalas crayfish
col cabbage
cuajada junket
embutidos sausages
emperador type of sword-fish
endivias chicory
ensalada salad
ensaladilla rusa Russian salad (diced potatoes and vegetables in mayonnaise)
entrecot steak
entremeses / fiambres hors d'œuvres / mixed cold meats
escalope escalope
escalope a la milanesa breaded veal escalope with cheese
escarola endive

espárragos asparagus
espinacas spinach
faisán pheasant
fideos noodles
filete fillet
flan crème caramel
frambuesas raspberries
fresas strawberries
fritura de pescado mixed fried fish
fruta fresh fruit
gallina hen
gambas prawns / shrimps
ganso goose
garbanzos chickpeas
guisantes peas
habas broad beans
habichuelas haricot beans
helado ice-cream
  mantecado vanilla ice-cream
hierbas herbs
hígado liver
hinojo fennel
huevas fish eggs / roe eggs
huevos eggs
  a la flamenca Andalusian style, baked with spicy sausage, tomato, peas, peppers, asparagus
  cocidos / duros hard-boiled eggs
  escalfados poached eggs
  huevos revueltos scrambled eggs
jabalí wild boar
jamón ham
  de york cooked ham
  serrano cured ham
judías beans
  blancas haricot beans
  verdes green / French beans
lacón type of cooked pork
langosta lobster
langostino king prawn
leche milk
  frita thick slices of custard fried in breadcrumbs
  merengada milk and meringue sorbet

lechuga lettuce
lengua tongue
lenguado sole
lentejas lentils
  aliñadas lentils with vinaigrette
liebre hare
lombarda red cabbage
lomo de cerdo loin of pork
longaniza type of spicy sausage
lubina sea bass
macarrones gratinados macaroni cheese
macedonia de frutas fruit salad
macedonia de verduras (mixed) vegetables
mahonesa mayonnaise
maíz sweetcorn
manos de cerdo pig's trotter
mantecada small sponge cake
mantequilla butter
mariscada mixed shellfish
mariscos seafood
mazapán marzipan
medallones small steaks
mejillones mussels
melón melon
membrillo quince jelly
menestra de verduras vegetable soup / stew
merluza hake
merluza a la gallega hake with paprika and tomatoes
mermelada jam
mermelada de naranja marmalade
miel honey
mixto/a mixed
moras blackberries
morcilla black pudding
mostaza mustard
nabo turnip
nata cream
natillas egg custard
nueces walnuts
ostras oysters
paella (valenciana) seafood risotto
paella catalana rice with sausage, pork, squid, tomato, peppers, peas

pan bread
  con tomate bread rubbed with garlic and fresh tomato
panaché de legumbres / verduras mixed vegetables
panceta bacon
parrillada mixed grill
pasas raisins
pastel cake
patatas potatoes
patatas fritas French fries
pato duck
  a la naranja duck in orange sauce
pavo turkey
pechuga de pollo chicken breast
pepinillo gherkin
pepino cucumber
perdiz partridge
perejil parsley
pescadilla whiting
pescado fish
pescaditos sprats
pez espada swordfish
picadillo minced meat / sausage
picatoste croutons
pimentón chilli pepper
pimienta pepper
pinchos morunos small kebabs
piñones pine kernels
pisto sautéed vegetable mix – courgettes, tomatoes, onions, peppers and aubergines
plato de fiambres mixed cold meats
pollo chicken
  en pepitoria chicken in a sauce of almonds, saffron, sherry and hard-boiled eggs
pomelo grapefruit
potaje thick vegetable soup
puerros leeks
pulpo octopus
puntas de espárragos asparagus tips
puré de patatas mashed potatoes
queso cheese
  de bola round, mild cheese (like Edam)
  de Burgos soft cream cheese from the Burgos area
  de cabra goat's milk cheese
  de Cabrales strong blue goat's

paella valenciana

cheese from northern Spain
de oveja sheep's milk cheese
fresco curd cheese
manchego hard cheese from la
Mancha, usually sheep's milk
quisquillas shrimps
rábano radish
rabo de buey oxtail
rape angler / monk fish
raya skate
remolacha beetroot
repollo cabbage
requesón curd / cream cheese
repostería pastries
riñones kidneys
rodaballo turbot
salami salami
salchicha sausage
salchichón salami-type sausage
salmón salmon
salmonete red mullet
salpicón de mariscos shellfish
with vinaigrette
salvia sage
samfaina mixture of onion,
tomato, peppers, aubergine and
courgette
sandía watermelon
sardinas sardines
sepia cuttlefish
sesos brains
setas wild mushrooms
sobrasada type of sausage (from
Mallorca)
solomillo fillet steak
sopa castellana vegetable soup
sopa de ajo garlic soup
sopa de almendra almond-based
pudding

sopa de picadillo chicken soup
with chopped sausage and egg
and noodles
sopa juliana vegetable soup
sorbete sorbet
tarta cake
al whisky whisky-flavoured ice-
cream gâteau
de manzana apple tart
ternera veal
tocinillo de cielo / tocinitos rich
crème caramel
tomate tomato
torrijas bread sliced, dipped in
beaten egg, fried and rolled in
sugar and cinnamon
tortilla omelette
a la paisana omelette with
mixed vegetables
francesa plain omelette
**española /
de patata**
Spanish
omelette
tostadas toast
trucha trout
uvas grapes
(carne de) vaca beef
vainilla vanilla
variados/as assorted
venado venison
verduras vegetables
vieiras scallops
yemas dessert of whipped egg
yolks, brandy and sugar
zanahorias carrots
**zarzuela de (pescados y)
mariscos** spicy (fish and)
seafood stew

Main sauces

a la crema creamed / in cream
sauce
ajillo / al ajillo with garlic and oil
alioli / allioli garlic mayonnaise
almíbar / en almíbar in syrup
(tinned)
bechamel béchamel sauce

blanca white
chilindrón / al chilindrón with dried
red peppers, tomato and ham
encebollado/a tomato with
onions / in onion sauce
gratinado/a with cheese topping /
au gratin

marinera / a la marinera in fish or seafood and tomato sauce
pil-pil / al pil-pil with chilli
romesca dried red peppers, almonds and garlic

verde green sauce, parsley, onion and garlic
vinagreta vinaigrette

(See p61 for fruits)

Drinks

agua del grifo tap water
agua mineral (con gas / sin gas) (sparkling / still) mineral water
aguardiente spirit
amontillado medium dry sherry
anís aniseed liqueur
aperitivo aperitif
batido milkshake
café (solo / cortado / con leche / descafeinado / con hielo) (black / slightly white / white / decaffeinated / iced) coffee
café irlandés Irish coffee
caña glass of draught beer
cava Spanish sparkling wine
cerveza beer
  de barril draught beer
  en botella bottled beer
  negra dark beer
  sin alcohol alcohol-free beer
champán champagne
chocolate caliente hot chocolate
chocolate frío cold chocolate
clara shandy
con crianza aged
coñac brandy
copa glass
corto small draught beer
cosecha vintage, year
cubalibre cubalibre (coke and white rum)
dulce sweet
embotellado por bottled by
espumoso sparkling
fino dry sherry
gaseosa lemonade
gin / ginebra gin
gintonic gin and tonic
granizado de (limón / melón) iced (lemon / melon) drink

hielo ice
horchata tiger-nut milk drink
infusión herbal tea
jerez sherry
manzanilla camomile tea
mosto grape juice
naranjada / limonada fizzy orange / lemon drink
oloroso strong, dark sherry
oporto port
poleo mint tea
reserva / gran reserva good / top quality wine
ron rum
sangría sangría
sidra cider
soda soda
sol y sombra brandy and aniseed liqueur
té tea
tinto de verano red wine and lemonade with ice
tónica tonic water
vermut vermouth
vino wine
  blanco white wine
  clarete light red wine
  de jerez sherry wine
  de la casa house wine
  de la tierra superior table wine
  del país local wine
  de mesa table wine
  rosado rosé wine
  tinto red wine
vodka vodka
whisky whisky
zumo de naranja orange juice

Entertainment and leisure

Finding out what's on

■ Spanish newspapers: the listings pages of local and national newspapers are clear and easy to understand even if your Spanish is limited. *El País* and *El Mundo* have detailed entertainment sections. In Madrid pick up a *Guia del Ocio* for a detailed guide to what's on.
■ Local tourist offices: staff are usually helpful, and can often give you translated brochures.
■ English-language newspapers: newspaper kiosks in tourist resorts and towns sell these locally edited weeklies advertising special events.

Spectator events

Bullfights The season runs from March to October and, like it or not, *Los toros* are an important part of the Spanish calendar, with the most popular matadors being millionaire household names.
The most famous bullring is Las

Ventas in Madrid, followed by Seville's Maestranza. Bullfights traditionally start at 5.00–7.00 pm to avoid the heat.
Football The Spanish are mad about football and if you can't make a live game, try and catch the atmosphere in a packed bar when there is an important match on TV. Top live venues are Real Madrid's Bernabeu Stadium, Atlético Madrid's Vicente Calderón Stadium, Barcelona's Nou Camp and Seville's Sánchez Pizjuán Stadium. The season runs from September to June and games are normally on Sundays.

❗ What is there to do here?
¿Qué se puede hacer aquí?

Fairs and festivals

The Spanish like a celebration, and their local fairs and festivals are a great opportunity to try out culinary specialities, or to watch traditional singing and dancing. Check tourist offices for details (see also Festivals p28).

Music

Tourist offices will give you details of classical, rock or jazz concerts and festivals. Don't miss typically Spanish shows such as:

■ **Flamenco** This guitar, singing and dancing is best heard in its native Andalusia, but can be just as impressive if you go to a flamenco club or bar in a major city or resort (see Madrid p5 and Sevilla p23).

■ **Salsa** and other Latin American rhythms are very popular in Spain. Head for a salsa club for an unforgettable night's dancing.

■ **Folk music** was outlawed under Franco's regime as a symbol of regional identity; it is now undergoing something of a resurgence. Galicia and Asturias are proud of their Celtic roots; try and catch such groups here or when they take their music on tours elsewhere. Regional language folk groups can also be found in Euskadi (Basque country), Cataluña, the Balearic Islands and Valencia.

Cinema

Spain's film industry has been highly successful recently with directors such as Pedro Almodóvar and Bigas Luna. Foreign films may be shown in the original language version, though many are dubbed into Spanish. Cinema tickets are relatively cheap and you can sometimes find mid-week reductions (*el día de las parejas*) offering two tickets for the price of one.

Sports

Skiing Spain has six well-equipped winter sports areas, in the Catalan Pyrenees, the Aragón Pyrenees, the Cantabrian Mountains, the Iberian range near La Rioja, the Central Range near Madrid and the exceptional range of Sierra Nevada in Granada. Many have on-site accommodation. The season lasts roughly from December to April, depending on the vagaries of winter.

Swimming The Mediterranean coasts are wonderful for safe swimming, especially in the May–September season. Few Spanish take a dip out of these months, considering the water too cold. Open-air pools open from mid-May to mid-September and are real oases for a few hours in the scorching summer

months, with patios or gardens, bars and restaurants.

Sailing There are about 250 mooring points for leisure craft around the Spanish coast where you can rent boats or yachts with or without crew. For information, check in local marinas or tourist offices.

Surfing This is big on the Cantabrian coast around Zarauz, where surf competitions are held, and at Tarifa on the south coast.

Walking There are over 1,226 square kilometres of spectacular National Parks which are ideal for walking. Try the waterfalls and glacial valleys of the Pyrenees. Other non-designated areas of mountain, beach and countryside can be just as appealing. Check with the nearest tourist office for local routes. Go on a week day, and you will probably meet no one on your ramble.

❗ Where are the changing rooms?
🔵 **¿Dónde están los vestuarios?**

Hunting Spain has a rich variety of fauna, so hunting is tightly controlled. The season starts in mid-October. Deer, chamois, wild boar and Spanish ibex as well as partridge, quail and duck are widely hunted, but check local tourist offices or the *Comunidades Autónomas* (regional regulating bodies) for details.

Fishing Sea fishing off the Mediterranean, Cantabrian and Atlantic coasts offers fish from mullet to tuna. Salmon, trout, pike and sturgeon are among the dozens of species lurking in over 75,000 km of inland rivers. Hunting and fishing licences can be obtained from the *Agencia de Medio Ambiente* in each regional capital.

Horseriding is generally considered a pastime of the wealthy. In reality, if you venture out into the villages, you can often find small riding schools charging a very reasonable rate. If you show you can handle a horse, it is possible to go out alone or in your own small party.

Golf There are over 102 courses in Spain, mostly on the Mediterranean coast, the islands and around Madrid. Almost all clubs give temporary permits to foreign visitors looking for a game.

Tennis Most cities, towns and resorts have public courts.

❗ Where can you play golf?
❗ **¿Dónde se puede jugar al golf?**

Phrasemaker
Getting to know the place

Do you have (a plan / map of the town / an entertainments guide)?	¿Tiene (un plano / un mapa de la ciudad / una guía de espectáculos)?
Do you have any information in English?	¿Tiene información en inglés?
Are there any (cinemas / concerts / nightclubs)?	¿Hay (cine / conciertos / nightclubs)?
What is there (to see / to do) here?	¿Qué se puede (ver / hacer) aquí?
Is there (a guided tour / a bus tour)?	¿Hay una visita (con guía / en autobús)?
Is there anything for children?	¿Hay algo para los niños?
Can you recommend a restaurant?	¿Puede recomendar un restaurante?

Hay una visita con guía (todos los días / los fines de semana).	There is a guided tour (every day / at weekends). (See Days of the week p36)
Está (cerca / lejos).	It's near / far.
Hay muchos monumentos interesantes.	There are lots of interesting sights.
¿Le gusta (el flamenco / la música / bailar)?	Do you like (flamenco / music / dancing)?
¿Qué le gusta?	What do you like?
Me gusta (la música clásica / la música pop / el fútbol).	I like (classical music / pop / football).
No me gustan (las corridas de toros / las discotecas).	I don't like (bullfights / discotheques).

Salamanca Cathedral

Things to do or see

castle	**el castillo / el alcázar**	bullfight	**una corrida de toros**
bridge	**el puente**	discotheque	**una discoteca**
river	**el río**	exhibition of	**una exposición**
fireworks	**fuegos artificiales**	(art / painting / ceramics)	**de (arte / pintura / cerámica)**
cathedral	**la catedral**	celebration	**una fiesta**
opera	**la ópera**	art gallery	**una galería de arte**
ticket-office	**la taquilla**		
cinema	**un cine**	swimming pool	**una piscina**
concert	**un concierto**	dance hall	**una sala de baile**
show	**un espectáculo**		
(music) festival	**un festival (de música)**	nightclub	**una sala de fiestas / un night-club**
monument	**un monumento**		
museum	**un museo**		
football match	**un partido de fútbol**		
theatre	**un teatro**		

MUSEO ARQUEOLOGICO

Getting more information

Where is (the swimming pool / the museum)?	**¿Dónde está (la piscina / el museo)?**
Where does the tour start?	**¿Dónde empieza la visita?**
What time does it (start / finish)?	**¿A qué hora (empieza / termina)?**
How much does it cost?	**¿Cuánto cuesta / vale?**
Are there any tickets for the concert?	**¿Hay entradas para el concierto?**
Do you need tickets?	**¿Se necesitan entradas?**
Where do you buy tickets?	**¿Dónde se compran las entradas?**

No se necesitan entradas.	You don't need tickets.
Es gratuita.	It's free.
Lo siento, están agotadas.	Sorry, it's sold out.
En la Plaza Mayor, a las diez.	In the main square, at 10 o'clock.
Desde las nueve y media de la mañana hasta las siete de la tarde	From 9.30 am to 7.00 pm
En la taquilla.	At the ticket office.
Aquí, en el plano.	Here, on the plan.

Getting in

Are there any tickets for (tonight / tomorrow)?	**¿Hay entradas para (esta noche / mañana)?**
How much are they?	**¿Cuánto valen?**
Two (stalls / circle) tickets, please.	**Dos entradas de (platea / anfiteatro).**
How long does it last?	**¿Cuánto tiempo dura?**
Does it have sub-titles?	**¿Tiene subtítulos?**
Is there an interval?	**¿Hay un descanso?**
Is this seat (taken / free)?	**¿Está (ocupado / libre) este asiento?**

Auditorio Nacional de Música, Madrid

entrada	entrance
guardarropa	cloakroom
lavabos / señoras / caballeros	toilets / ladies / gentlemen
platea	stalls
anfiteatro	circle
'paraíso'	'gods'
escalera	stairs
bar / café	bar / café
un programa	a programme
salida	exit

Sports

skis	**los esquíes**
the beach	**la playa**
golf clubs	**los palos de golf**
balls	**las pelotas**
golf course	**un campo de golf**
boat	**una barca**
table	**una mesa**
tennis court	**una pista de tenis**
chair	**una silla**
sunshade	**una sombrilla**
towel	**una toalla**

Where can you play (tennis / golf)?	**¿Dónde se puede jugar al (tenis / golf)?**
Where can you (sail / surf)?	**¿Dónde se puede hacer (vela / surfing)?**
Where can you go (walking / climbing)?	**¿Dónde se puede hacer (excursiones / alpinismo)?**
to fish	**hacer pesca**
to water-ski	**hacer esquí acuático**
to wind-surf	**hacer wind-surf**
Can I hire (a tennis racket / a wind-surf board / water-skis)?	**¿Se puede alquilar (una raqueta de tenis / una plancha / esquíes acuáticos)?**
I'd like to take sailing lessons.	**Quisiera tomar clases de vela.**
Where are (the changing rooms / the showers)?	**¿Dónde están (los vestuarios / las duchas)?**

Language works

Getting to know the place

1 You find out about Salamanca in the Tourist Office

- ¿Qué se puede ver en Salamanca?
- ☐ Pues, hay muchos monumentos interesantes, la Catedral Nueva y la Catedral Vieja, el puente romano.
- ¿Hay conciertos de música clásica?
- ☐ Sí, sobre todo los fines de semana.
- Gracias.

(**sobre todo** = especially)

Roman Bridge, Salamanca

You can hear classical music at weekends: true or false?
The receptionist mentions nightclubs: true or false?

Deciding what to do

2 The receptionist is keen to help

- Hay una corrida el domingo.
- ☐ No me gustan las corridas. ¿Hay exposiciones de cerámica?
- Sí, en el Museo de Cerámica.
- ☐ ¿Dónde está?
- Está cerca.

What could you see on Sunday?
Where can you see ceramics?

Getting more information

3 You decide on a nightclub

- ¿Dónde está la sala de fiestas 'La Sevillana'?
- ☐ Está en la calle de Serrano, aquí en el mapa.
- Y ¿a qué hora abre?
- ☐ A las once, aproximadamente.
- Y ¿se necesitan entradas?
- ☐ No. La entrada es gratuita.

'La Sevillana' opens at about eight / eleven / one o'clock.
You do / do not need to buy tickets.

Sport

4 You decide to test the water

- ¿Se puede hacer wind-surf aquí?
- ☐ Sí. ¿Quiere tomar alguna clase?
- ¿Cuánto cuesta?
- ☐ Tres mil pesetas.
- Muy bien.

How much is a wind-surf lesson?

Sound Check

c
When a **c** in Spanish is *not* followed by an **e** or an **i** it is pronounced like the 'c' at the start of the English 'cool'.

concierto	konthee-erto
cerámica	therameeka

Practise with these words:
corrida, flamenco, recomendar, descanso, catedral

Try it out

Crossword/Crucigrama

Horizontales

1 ¿Hay ..... para esta noche?
4 Una ..... de fiestas
6 ¿Qué ..... es el partido, el sábado? No, el domingo.
8 ¿..... ..... hora empieza el concierto?
9 Hay fiesta todos ..... días.
11 ¿Hay entradas para esta .....?

Verticales

2 ¿..... se compran las entradas?
3 El ..... y el domingo son los días del fin de semana
4 Una ..... de baile
5 ¿Dónde es ..... fiesta del domingo?
6 Hay una exposición ..... pintura
7 ¿Dónde ..... compran las entradas?
9 ¿..... gusta el baile?
   No, pero me gusta la música.
10 ¿Le gusta la cerámica?
   ....., mucho.

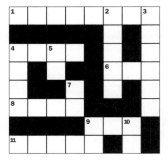

As if you were there

You are looking for a way to spend a Sunday in Cáceres, so you talk to a lady in the *Oficina de Turismo* (Tourist Office).

■ (Greet her and ask what there is to do in Cáceres)
□ **Pues hay una corrida de toros. ¿Le gustan los toros?**
■ (No. Are there any fiestas?)
□ **Sí, hay una fiesta de baile regional aquí en la Plaza Mayor.**
■ (Ask what time it starts)
□ **A las diez de la mañana.**
■ (What about tonight?)
□ **Hay cines, un concierto de música clásica, también hay fuegos artificiales a las once.**
■ (Find out where you can get tickets for the concert)
□ **Aquí, son de dos mil pesetas.**

What's happening in the Main Square this morning?
What three choices are you offered for this evening?
Where can you get tickets for the concert, and how much are they?

Emergencies

POLICIA LOCAL
LOCAL POLICE

Crime

Violent crime is rare in Spain, but petty crime – pick-pocketing and bag-snatching – is more widespread, especially in cities and in tourist areas. It is advisable to take reasonable precautions wherever you go. Leave valuables, including passport and air tickets, in a secure place such as the hotel safe. Take a photocopy of your passport and carry it with you (you will need it to change money, and technically in Spain you should have some form of ID with you at all times). Use a bag with a long strap that you can cross over your shoulders especially for sightseeing or wandering around crowded markets, on public transport or in packed bars. Alternatively, take just as much money as you need in deep, hidden pockets. Never leave valuables unattended in tents or on the beach when you go for a dip. Women travelling alone are unlikely to be attacked but should take special care especially in out-of-the-way places, or anywhere at night.

As in any major city, be particularly vigilant when travelling on the metro in Barcelona and Madrid.

Police help
If you are robbed do not resist – armed thieves usually mean business. Report the incident to the nearest police station immediately. It is unlikely that the police will find the culprit and recoup your belongings, but you can ask for a written report for insurance purposes.

There are three types of police. The *Policía Municipal*, in blue and white uniforms with a red trim, deal with any crimes in their region, especially smaller offences (such as a bag snatching). The *Policía Nacional*, in brown uniforms, deal with more serious crimes such as robberies and rape; they also guard key government buildings. The *Guardia Civil*, in green uniforms, deal with security on the roads and collect on-the-spot fines for traffic offences. Do not confuse the police with the armed security guards that stand imposingly around the doors and foyers of most private companies, banks and in the metro.

❗ Where's the nearest police station?
🔴 ¿Dónde está la comisaría más cercana?

Health matters

AGUA NO POTABLE

You do not need any innoculations, and food and drinking water is generally safe. Certain areas, such as Barcelona or Málaga, have salty tap water so get bottled water in bars and restaurants. Bottled mineral water is cheap if you buy it in shops or super-markets. Avoid drinking from taps in public toilets or out-of-the-way places. If you travel in summer, take care when choosing which *tapas* to sample. Most Spaniards avoid egg- and mayonnaise-based dishes, which can quickly spoil in the heat. Go for bars and restaurants with refrigerated displays.

Toilets

ASEOS

Public toilets are few and far between, though some large parks, and all public buildings, art galleries and museums have clean, modern facilities. Toilets are marked *aseos* or *servicios: mujeres / señoras / M* for women or *hombres / señores / caballeros / H* for men.

Nip into large and busy *cafeterías* or *cervecerías* if you cannot find a public loo, no one tends to notice or mind even if you do not stay for a drink.

Nasties

There are poisonous snakes and insects with nasty bites and stings, but they are unlikely to catch up with you. Take sensible precautions if you go hiking, wearing decent boots and socks even in summer. Mosquitoes and flies can be a pain in some areas; use a repellent if you are venturing out into the country. To avoid sunburn, avoid the midday sun, always wear sun cream and, ideally, a hat.

Medical treatment

If you fall ill, go to the nearest *farmacia*, where they will recommend the appropriate treatment. In every town and most city *barrios*, there is a *farmacia de guardia* (emergency chemist) open 24 hours. Check in the local papers tourist office or outside any chemist

FARMACIA

for the list showing the address and phone number of the nearest one. You can usually consult the chemist for advice and many prescription-type tablets and medicines such as antibiotics are available over the counter.

If the matter is more serious, they will refer you to the nearest clinic (*ambulatorio*). Be prepared for a long wait and fairly brusque treatment. You will also probably have to pay, but you should be able to claim it back on insurance (make sure they give you all the necessary paperwork). Dial 191 or 192 for emergency services. EU nationals with form E111 (available before the trip from post offices in the country of origin) are entitled to free emergency treatment.

CLINICA PUERTO J. BANUS DR. GOMEZ AGUILAR TLF. 281 39 35

I'd like to speak to a doctor.
Quisiera hablar con un médico.

Telephones

Even the smallest towns and villages have a public phone, often inside a bar or cafeteria. Modern plastic-hooded phones are generally replacing older *cabinas* (telephone kiosks). The most modern accept major credit cards, phone cards (*tarjetas telefónicas*) and new denomination coins. You can purchase phone cards in an *estanco* in units of 1000 or 2000 pesetas. Older phones and those more off the beaten track (there are plenty) only accept old 5pta, 25pta and old 100pta coins. Most call boxes have illustrations for use, and phones with facilities for international calls have instructions in several languages as well as world-wide country codes. Major centres have telephone offices where you call from a cabin; you speak and pay later on a price-per-unit basis.

Post office facilities

Correos are found in every town and city and accept poste restante *(apartado de correos)* mail for a small fee. Smaller villages have a post box for posting mail, but you can buy stamps (*sellos*) in the *estanco*. Post boxes are yellow and marked with a horn symbol. There is usually an area for posting marked on the exterior wall of the main post office: Madrid, *provincias* (rest of Spain) and *extranjero* (abroad).

Useful telephone numbers

Emergencies 191 (national) 192 (local)
Fire brigade 080
Directory enquiries 003
International directory enquiries 025

Embassies in Spain
■ Australian Embassy: Paseo de la Castellana 143, 28046 Madrid. Tel: (91) 579 0428.
■ British Embassy: C/ Fernando el Santo 16, Madrid. Tel: (91) 319 0200. Consulate: Edificio Colón, Marqués de la Ensenada 16, Madrid. Tel: (91) 308 5201.
■ Canadian Embassy: Edificio Goya, C/ Nuñez de Balboa, 35 Madrid. Tel: (91) 423 3250.
■ Irish Embassy: C/ Claudio Coello 73, Madrid. Tel: (91) 436 4093.
■ New Zealand Embassy: Plaza de la Lealtad, 2, 3rd floor, 28014 Madrid. Tel: (91) 523 0226.
■ South African Embassy: Claudio Coello 91, Madrid. Tel: 435 66 88.
■ US Embassy: C/Serrano, 51 Madrid. Tel: (91) 577 4000.

There are additional consulates in other major cities and resorts such as Barcelona, Seville, Tenerife and Mallorca.

Central Post Office, Madrid

Phrasemaker
Getting help – and showing thanks

HELP!	**¡SOCORRO!**
Watch out!	**¡Cuidado!**
Hello there!	**¡Oiga!**
Excuse me!	**¡Por favor!**
Can you help me?	**¿Me puede ayudar?**
Where is the nearest (police station / garage)?	**¿Dónde está (la comisaría más cercana / el garaje más cercano)?**

I need (a doctor / an ambulance).	**Necesito (un médico / una ambulancia).**
It's urgent.	**Es urgente.**
Do you speak English?	**¿Habla usted inglés?**
I'd like to speak to (a doctor / a dentist).	**Quisiera hablar con (un médico / un dentista).**
Thank you (very much).	**(Muchas) gracias.**
Don't mention it.	**De nada.**
Leave me alone!	**¡Déjeme en paz!**
I'll call the police!	**¡Llamaré a la policía!**

Talking to a doctor or a dentist

I have a sore (throat / neck).	**Me duele (la garganta / el cuello).**
(My eyes / My feet) ache.	**Me duelen (los ojos / los pies).**
It hurts (a lot / a bit / here).	**Me duele (mucho / un poco / aquí).**

Some common aches and pains and complaints

I've got a headache.	**Me duele la cabeza.**
I've got a sore throat.	**Me duele la garganta.**
This tooth hurts.	**Me duele esta muela.**
I've got earache.	**Me duele el oído.**
I've got a stiff neck.	**Me duele el cuello.**
I've got backache.	**Me duele la espalda.**
I've got a cold.	**Estoy constipado/constipada.** *
I've got constipation.	**Estoy estreñido/estreñida.** *
I've got diarrhoea.	**Tengo diarrea.**
I've got a cough.	**Tengo tos.**
I've got sunburn.	**Tengo quemaduras del sol.**
I've got a broken (leg / arm).	**Tengo (la pierna rota / el brazo roto).**
I've been sick.	**He vomitado.**
I've cut my (leg / finger).	**Me he cortado (la pierna / el dedo).**
I can't move my (arm / leg).	**No puedo mover (el brazo / la pierna).**
I have asthma.	**Tengo asma.**
I'm allergic to antibiotics.	**Soy alérgico/a a los antibióticos.** *
I'm pregnant.	**Estoy en estado.**
I'm diabetic.	**Soy diabético/diabética.** *
I wear contact lenses.	**Llevo lentes de contacto.**
My (son / daughter) has a temperature.	**Mi (hijo / hija) tiene fiebre.**
(He/she) is allergic.	**Es (alérgico/alérgica).** *

No es grave.	It's not serious.
Tiene un hueso roto.	You have a broken bone.
Hay que operar.	You need an operation.
Esta es una receta.	This is a prescription.
Voy a (empastar / sacar) la muela.	I'm going (to fill / take out) the tooth.

*Where two words are given, the one ending in
-a is used to describe females, the one in **-o** by males.

Parts of the body

arm	**el brazo**	head	**la cabeza**
shoulder	**el codo**	hip	**la cadera**
the body	**el cuerpo**	hand	**la mano**
thigh	**el muslo**	nose	**la nariz**
(inner) ear	**el oído**	(outer) ear	**la oreja**
chest	**el pecho**	leg	**la pierna**
foot	**el pie**	knee	**la rodilla**
thumb	**el pulgar**	kidneys	**los riñones**
ankle	**el tobillo**	eyes	**los ojos**
mouth	**la boca**	liver	**el hígado**

At the chemist's

Do you have anything for . . .	**¿Tiene algo para . . .**
. . . a cough?	**. . . la tos?**
. . . a headache?	**. . . el dolor de cabeza?**
. . . constipation?	**. . . el estreñimiento?**
. . . sunburn?	**. . . las quemaduras del sol?**
. . . bites?	**. . . las picaduras?**
Do you have . . .	**¿Tiene . . .**
. . . aspirin?	**aspirina?**
. . . after sun lotion?	**after-sun?**
. . . antihistamine?	**antihistamínico?**
. . . baby food?	**alimento para bebés?**
. . . contact-lens solution?	**solución para lentes de contacto?**
. . . condoms?	**condones / preservativos?**
. . . cough mixture?	**un jarabe?**
. . . nappies?	**pañales?**
. . . a sticking plaster?	**una caja de tiritas?**
. . . sanitary towels?	**paños higiénicos / compresas?**
. . . a laxative?	**un laxante?**

¿Le duele mucho?	Does it hurt a lot?
Tome este jarabe.	Take this syrup / mixture.
Tome (estas pastillas / estos antibióticos).	Take these (pills / antibiotics).
Aplíquese esta (pomada / crema) . . .	Put on this (cream) . . .
en seguida.	straight away.
una vez al día.	once a day.
tres veces al día.	three times a day.
cada cuatro horas.	every four hours.
(antes / después) de las comidas.	(before / after) meals.
Debe (descansar / dormir).	You must (rest / sleep).
No debe (salir / levantarse).	You mustn't (go out / get up).

Car breakdown

I'm on the road number N26.	**Estoy en la carretera número N26.**
I'm 15 kilometres from Ronda.	**Estoy a quince kilómetros de Ronda.**
At kilometre 110	**En el kilómetro ciento diez**
I have a breakdown.	**Tengo una avería.**
The car has a flat tyre.	**El coche tiene un pinchazo.**
The engine isn't working.	**El motor no (funciona / arranca).**
starter	**el motor de arranque**
battery	**la batería**
The lights aren't working.	**Las luces no funcionan.**
How long will they be?	**¿Cuánto tardarán?**
When will it be ready?	**¿Cuándo estará listo?**

¿Qué le pasa?	What's the matter?
¿Cuál es su (mátricula / nombre)?	What's your (registration number / name)?
Ahora mismo / En seguida	Straight away
En dos horas	In two hours

Lost or stolen

I've lost my (wallet / passport).	**He perdido mi (cartera / pasaporte).**
I've had my watch stolen.	**Me han robado el reloj.**
This (morning / evening)	**Esta (mañana / tarde)**
In (the street / a shop)	**En (la calle / una tienda)**
I think	**Creo**
I don't know.	**No sé.**

briefcase	**un maletín**	suitcase	**una maleta**
handbag	**un bolso**	driving licence	**el permiso de conducir**
necklace	**un collar**	jewellery	**las joyas**
purse	**un monedero**	money	**el dinero**
ring	**una sortija / un anillo**	tickets	**los billetes**

¿Cuándo?	When?
¿Dónde?	Where?
¿Qué?	What?
¿Nombre?	Name?
(El pasaporte / El documento de identidad), por favor.	(Your passport / identity document), please.
Rellene esta hoja.	Fill in this form.
Vuelva mañana.	Come back tomorrow.

Language works

A helping hand

1 You see a child with its mother who appears about to step in front of an oncoming motorbike
- ¡Cuidado!
- □ Muchas gracias.
- De nada.

How does the mother react?

At the doctor's (1)

2 You explain about a stomach problem
- Me duele el estómago.
- □ ¿Está estreñida?
- No, tengo un poco de diarrea.
- □ No es grave. Tome este jarabe cada cuatro horas.

The doctor thinks it's serious: true/false?
You take the medicine every four hours: true/false?

At the doctor's (2)

3 Your daughter is not well
- Mi hija tiene fiebre

- □ ¿Tiene dolor de cabeza?
- Sí.
- □ No es grave. Debe descansar dos días.
- Muy bien. Gracias.

What should she do?

Getting help from the chemist (1)

4 Your throat is troubling you
- Me duele la garganta.
- □ Tome estas pastillas, dos cada tres horas.

How often do you have to take the pills?

Getting help from the chemist (2)

5 Sunburn strikes
- ¿Tiene algo para las quemaduras del sol?
- □ ¿Le duele mucho?
- Sí.
- □ Aplíquese esta pomada en seguida.
- Muchas gracias.

What do you have to do?

Transport problems

6 You walk to a garage to report a breakdown
- Buenos días. Tengo una avería.
- □ ¿Dónde está su coche?
- En el kilómetro sesenta y cinco.
- □ ¿Qué le pasa?
- El motor no arranca. ¿Me puede ayudar?
- □ Sí, ahora mismo.

How soon can you get help?

Lost property

7 You've lost your wallet – again!
- He perdido mi cartera.

□ **¿Dónde?**
■ **En la calle, creo.**
□ **Rellene esta hoja y vuelva mañana.**

What do you have to do?

Sound Check

g
When a **g** in Spanish is followed by an **e** or an **i** it is pronounced like the 'ch' in the Scottish pronunciation of 'loch'.

ginebra	hheenebra
urgente	oorrhhentey

Practise with these words:
alérgico, general

When a **g** in Spanish is followed by anything else it is pronounced like the 'g' in 'go'.

garganta	garganta
garaje	garahhey

Practise with these words: **oiga, gracias, hígado, pulgar, en seguida**

Try it out

Helplink

1 Match each of the seven phrases with the most suitable response.
1 ¿Me puede ayudar?
2 ¿Qué le pasa?
3 ¡Muchas gracias!
4 ¿Tardarán mucho?
5 ¿Dónde está su coche?
6 ¿Tiene algo para el dolor de cabeza?

a De nada.
b En la carretera de Madrid.
c Me duelen las muelas.
d Sí, tome estas aspirinas.
e Sí, claro.
f No, unos momentos.

2 Link each of the ten phrases with the most suitable continuation.
1 ¿Tiene algo para
2 Tengo dolor de
3 Tome estas
4 ¿Qué le
5 Me duelen
6 ¿Tiene un
7 El motor de arranque
8 Debe
9 He perdido
10 Soy alérgico/a a

a ls ojos
b pasa?
c no funciona
d descansar
e esparadrapo?
f la tos?
g pastillas
h cabeza
i los antibióticos
j mi pasaporte

As if you were there

You're not feeling well, so you go to a chemist's shop.
■ (You say good morning)
□ **Buenos días**
■ (Explain you have sunburn)
□ **¿Le duele la cabeza?**
■ (A little, and you've been sick)
□ **Aplíquese esta pomada. Y debe descansar.**
■ (Thank her very much)
□ **De nada.**

What two things do you have to do?

Language builder

Gender

All Spanish nouns (words used for people and things) are either feminine or masculine. A word's gender affects:
– the form of 'a' and 'the' used before it
– any adjectives used with it

Masculine words usually end in **-o**
– **teléfono, estanco.**
Feminine words usually end in **-a**
– **revista, farmacia.**

'a' and 'the': the articles

'a'
Feminine: **una**
una cerveza (a beer)

Masculine: **un**
un vaso (a glass)

un periódico (a newspaper)
una revista (a magazine)
un estanco (a tobacconist's, a stamp shop)
una frutería (a fruit shop)
un supermercado (a supermarket)
una botella (a bottle)

'the'

Feminine: **la**
la camisa (the shirt)

Masculine: **el**
el vestido (the dress)

Plural feminine: **las**
las camisas (the shirts)

Plural masculine: **los**
los vestidos (the dresses)

Singular and plural

When you are talking about more than one person or thing, you normally:

– add an '**s**' to the word if it ends in a vowel (especially **a**, **e**, or **o**)
una pera (one pear)
dos peras (two pears)
un plátano (one banana)
dos plátanos (two bananas)
un albaricoque (one apricot)
dos albaricoques (two apricots)
– add '**es**' if it ends in a consonant (ie any other letter)
un señor (one gentleman)
dos señores (two gentlemen)
un limón (one lemon)
dos limones (two lemons)

When you learn a word, learn it with the word for 'a' and 'the'. Example: You learn the words **cereza** (cherry) and **melón** (melon) As you do, you learn also
Una cereza, la cereza, las cerezas – a cherry, the cherry, the cherries ('cherry' is feminine)
Un melón, el melón, los melones – a melon, the melon, the melons ('melon' is masculine)

Talking to people

In Spanish you need to use a different verb form depending on who you're talking to and whether it's
– to one person, or to more than one
– to someone you know a little bit, or to a complete stranger you want to be polite to.

Here are the different ways you would ask 'Do you speak English?'

¿Habla usted inglés?
(To one person you haven't met before)
¿Hablan ustedes inglés?
(To more than one you haven't met before)
¿Hablas tú inglés?
(To one person you are friendly with)
¿Habláis vosotros* inglés?
(To a group of people you are friendly with)

*In this last one, if they were all female, you would use **vosotras.**

If in doubt, imagine at first that you're speaking to someone you don't know too well – because as a visitor you usually are anyway! This means you use the word **usted** (one person) or **ustedes** (more than one person).

The word you use will often affect the word or words (verbs) that follow. So read on . . .

Verbs

Verbs, which are usually actions, change their endings quite often in Spanish. The things that make the endings change are:
– who is doing the action (the person).
– how many of them there are (singular/plural).
– when they did or are doing it.

¿Cuánto <u>vale</u> el melón?
How much does the melon cost?
¿Cuánto <u>valen</u> las peras?
How much do the melons cost?
<u>Tengo</u> (un) catarro.
I have a cold.
Mi hija <u>tiene</u> (un) catarro.
My daughter has a cold.

From this you will see that verbs and their endings change in

English too! (does, do, have, has) And if you want to go a little bit further, here is the whole Present tense of the verb **hablar** (to speak)

(Yo) hablo
I speak
(Tú) hablas
You* speak (informal)
(El/ella) habla
He/she speaks
(Usted) habla
You* speak (more formal)
(Nosotros) hablamos
We speak
(Vosotros/vosotras) habláis
You* speak
(Ellos/ellas) hablan
They speak
(Ustedes) hablan
You* speak

*For the different meanings of 'You' see the explanation Talking to people.

Keep your eyes open for the different endings that you meet of the same verb. Collect them, and try to form patterns.

Adjectives

An adjective changes form according to whether it refers to:
– a masculine or feminine word
– a singular or plural word

Like nouns, adjectives often end in **-o/-a** in the singular and **-os/-as** in the plural.

Singular
un museo <u>moderno</u>
a modern museum
una iglesia <u>moderna</u>
a modern church
El museo es <u>moderno</u>.
The museum is modern.
La iglesia es <u>moderna</u>.
The church is modern.

Plural
manzanas <u>amarillas</u>
yellow apples
Las manzanas son <u>amarillas</u>.
The apples are yellow.
pimientos <u>rojos</u>
red peppers
Los pimientos son <u>rojos</u>.
The peppers are red.

When you are describing things,
try to make an 'echo' between
the thing or person you are
describing and the word used to
describe it.

eg
**¿Hay un restaurante <u>bueno</u> por
aquí?**
Is there a good restaurant round
here?
¿Es <u>antigua</u> la iglesia?
Is the church old?
Los calamares están muy <u>ricos</u>.
The squid are delicious.
Déme un kilo de uvas <u>verdes</u>.
A kilo of green grapes please.

Note the order of words when an
adjective is put with a noun
– **manzanas amarillas**
– **pimientos rojos**
– **una iglesia antigua**
– **un museo moderno.**
In English the adjective normally
comes first, in Spanish it's
usually the noun. Simple!

Questions

There are two ways to ask a
question.

1 Usually you just turn the
statement around:
El mercado está cerca.
The market is close.
*****¿Está cerca el mercado?**
Is the market close?

2 Use the same form as for the
statement but with a question
intonation:
Tiene manzanas.
You have some apples.
*****¿Tiene manzanas?**
Do you have any apples?

The difference is clear when you
speak, because of the rise in
your voice, and because of the
situation (you're not likely to be
telling a stallholder he has some
apples!).
*Note the upside-down question
marks. Fortunately, when you're
speaking they don't make any
difference!

Talking about possessions

de (of) is used to show
possession:
My husband's suitcase
La maleta <u>de</u> mi marido

De is also used in Spanish in
several cases where in English we
simply use a different word order:

el grifo <u>del</u> agua caliente
the hot-water tap
el Museo <u>del</u> Prado
the Prado Museum
una entrada <u>de</u> teatro
a theatre ticket
el autobús <u>de</u> Salamanca
the Salamanca bus, the bus to
Salamanca

There are special words for
personal possession. They are
adjectives (see above), so they
all change according to what they
refer to.
eg my watch – **<u>mi</u> reloj**
my glasses – **<u>mis</u> gafas**

	Singular	Plural
my	**mi**	**mis**
your*	**su**	**sus**
	tu	**tus**
	vuestro	**vuestras**
his	**su**	**sus**
our	**nuestro**	**nuestras**
their	**su reloj**	**sus**

*For the different meanings of 'You' see the explanation Talking to people on p108.

This, that, these, those

These words behave like adjectives so they have different forms, depending on what they refer to:
este melón/estos melones
this melon/these melons
esta sandía/estas sandías
this water-melon/these water-melons
ese melón/esos melones
that melon/those melons
esa sandía/esas sandías
that water-melon/those water-melons

Things you like: *gustar*

To talk about what you like and dislike in Spanish, you need the phrases **me gusta** and **me gustan**.
<u>**Me gusta** el vino tinto, <u>no me gusta</u> el vino blanco.</u>
I like red wine, I don't like white wine.
<u>**Me gustan** las alcachofas, <u>no me gustan</u> las berenjenas.</u>
I like artichokes, I don't like aubergines.

What the Spaniards actually say is 'Red wine is pleasing to me. Artichokes are pleasing to me'. So when you're talking about **one** thing, you use the singular form **me gusta** and when you're talking

about more than one, the plural form **me gustan**.

Try to remember that **gustar** means 'to please', and take it from there.

Pronouns

From some of the examples above, you will see that in Spanish you often drop the word for 'I', 'you', 'he', 'she', 'they', and 'it'.
So you usually say:
Hablo inglés – I speak English, instead of **Yo hablo inglés**
¿Tiene aceite? – Do you have any oil?, instead of **¿Tiene usted aceite?**

If in doubt, use the pronoun. You will always be understood. So you can say **Yo hablo inglés** – even though you might not hear it very much.

The verbs 'to be'

There are two words that mean 'is', 'am', 'are' in Spanish. They are **ser** and **estar**.
¿Dónde <u>está</u> la Plaza Mayor?
Where is the Main Square?
<u>**Está** al final de la calle.</u>
It's at the end of the street.
Here you use **está** because you're talking about where something is.

¿Cómo <u>es</u> la Plaza Mayor?
What is the Main Square like?
<u>**Es** magnífica.</u>
It's magnificent.
Here you use **es** because you're talking about what something is like.

Keep it simple. The above rule applies to the vast majority of cases.

Answers

Bare necessities
1 Afternoon; 55 pesetas
2 4.625 pesetas; your passport

What to say when
1 ¿Hay servicios?
2 Buenas tardes.
3 ¿A qué hora abren?
4 Por favor / Con permiso
5 ¿Dónde esta el Hotel San Jorge?
6 ¿Quiere repetir eso?
7 ¿Tiene gasolina sin plomo?
8 ¿Cuánto es?

As if you were there
■ Por favor.
■ Buenos días.
■ ¿Dónde esta el banco?
■ ¿A qué hora cierran?
■ Muchas gracias.
■ Adiós.

Getting around
1 the end of the street/left;
2 7.500 pesetas; 3 30 kilometres
(approximately); 4 11.20 and 13.10; 9;
20 minutes; 5 more (650 pesetas)

Picture this
1 e; 2 d; 3 f; 4 c; 5 b; 6 a

Crossed lines
■ ¿La estación de ferrocarril, por favor?
□ La primera a la izquierda.
■ ¿Está lejos?
□ No, a unos setecientos metros.
■ Gracias.

■ ¿A qué hora sale el tren para Valencia?
□ A las nueve treinta.
■ ¿De qué andén?
□ Andén cinco.
■ Gracias.

As if you were there
■ ¿Hay autobuses para Salamanca?
■ ¿Cuándo sale el autobús?
■ ¿Cuánto tarda?
■ Dos billetes de ida y vuelta.

Somewhere to stay
1 9.000 pesetas; 2 True; False;
3 16.100 pesetas; Show your passport and fill in a form; 4 2nd, 1st;
5 8 am, 9.30 pm; 6 Yes, hopefully!;
7 True; True; 8 Yes

All the As
1 habitación; 2 reserva; 3 llave;
4 cama; 5 pasaporte; 6 ascensor;
7 escalera; 8 restaurante;
9 desayuno; 10 cena; 11 ducha;
12 agua

Mix up
M; J; C; D; N; F; G; L; I; B; K; H; A; E

Buying things
1 160 pesetas; 2 She liked them;
3 Most expensive – ham; least –
pineapple juice; 4 180 pesetas;
5 Tomorrow afternoon

Syllable salad
zumo, plátano, jamón, melocotón,
alcachofa, queso, huevo, sardina,
naranja, cereza

Mix and match
1 e; 2 f; 3 h; 4 a; 5 b; 6 d; 7 g; 8 c

As if you were there
■ Buenos días.
■ Cien gramos de chorizo y doscientos
gramos de jamón serrano.
■ ¿Tiene pan?
■ Una barra grande.
■ Nada más, gracias. ¿Cuánto es?
■ Aquí tiene. Gracias, adiós.

Café life
1 True; Pineapple juice, orange juice,
horchata; 2 Squid and prawns;
820 pesetas; 3 Ham, cheese, chorizo
(sausage), tuna and Spanish omelette;
4 Brandy

Mixing them
Una copa de coñac
Un vaso de tinto
Una botella de cava
Una caña
Una media caña
Una ración de calamares
Una taza de té
Un fino

Allergies
a Gambas a la plancha; sardinas; anchoas; mejillones; caracoles de mar; boquerones
b Queso manchego; ensaladilla rusa; tortilla española;
c Chorizo, empanadillas de carne

Split the difference
zumo, gaseosa, café, cerveza, helado, cava, descafeinado, granizado, sangría, ginebra

As if you were there
■ Buenas tardes. Una cerveza, un vermú y un vino blanco.
■ ¿Qué tapas tienen?
■ Una ración de jamón, (una ración) de boquerones, y una (ración) de tortilla.
■ ¡Oiga!, camarero ¿Cuánto es?

Eating out
1 A drink; 2 Besugo al horno (Baked sea bream); 3 Sparkling; 4 Two; 5 How the meal was

Sopa de letras
hors-d'œuvres – entremeses; salad – ensalada; seafood – mariscos; squid – calamares; beer – cerveza; octopus – pulpo; wild boar – jabalí; prawns – gambas; dessert – postre; garlic – ajo; soup – sopa; cod – bacalao; pork – cerdo
rica; rico; plato

Menu-making
Primer plato: Ensalada de atún, Crema de espárragos, Gambas a la plancha, Jamón serrano, Pimientos rellenos, Riñones al jerez, Champiñones al ajillo
Plato principal: Arroz a la cubana, Besugo al horno, Solomillo, Perdiz 'El Bosque'
Postre: Flan, Membrillo, Helados mixtos

As if you were there
■ Buenas noches. Una mesa para dos.
■ Un vaso de vino tinto y un fino.
■ ¿Cómo son las 'langostas a la santanderina'?
■ Dos de langosta, una sopa de cebolla y una ensalada mixta.
■ ¡Muy rica!
■ No, la cuenta por favor.

Entertainment and leisure
1 True; False; 2 A bullfight; The Pottery Museum; 3 Eleven; do not; 4 3.000 pesetas

A sporting chance
1 barca; 2 palos de golf; 3 vela; 4 raqueta; 5 pelota; 6 esquí

Crossword / Crucigrama
Across 1 entradas; 4 sala; 6 día; 8 a que; 9 los; 11 noche
Down 2 Donde; 3 sábado; 4 sala; 5 la; 6 de; 7 se; 9 Le; 10 Si

As if you were there
■ Buenos días, ¿Qué hay para hacer en Cáceres?
■ No. ¿Hay fiestas?
■ ¿A qué hora empieza?
■ ¿Y esta noche?
■ ¿Dónde se compran las entradas?

1 A regional dance festival
2 Cinema, classical music concert, fireworks
3 At the Tourist Information office; 2.000 pesetas

Emergencies
1 She thanks you; 2 False; True; 3 Rest for two days; 4 Two every three hours; 5 Put the cream on straight away; 6 Straight away; 7 Fill in the form and come back tomorrow

Helplink
1 1 f; 2 h; 3 g; 4 b; 5 a; 6 e; 7 c; 8 d; 9 j; 10 i
2 1 e; 2 c; 3 a; 4 f; 5 b; 6 d

As if you were there
■ Buenos días.
■ Tengo quemaduras del sol.
■ Un poco, y he vomitado.
■ Muchas gracias.

Put some cream on and rest.

Dictionary

a la parrilla grilled
a la plancha griddled
a la romana in batter/deep fried
a punto medium (steak)
abren open
abrigo, el coat
abrir to open
aceite, el oil
aceituna, la olive
aceptar to take/accept
adios goodbye
adulto/a adult
aeropuerto, el airport
after-sun, el after-sun lotion
agencia, la agency
agotado/a sold out
agua mineral (con gas/sin gas), el mineral water sparkling/still)
agua, el water
aguacate, el avocado
aguardiente, el spirit
ahora now
ahora mismo straight away
ahumado/a smoked
aire acondicionado, el air conditioning
aire, el air
ajo, el garlic
al adobo marinated
al horno in the oven/baked
albaricoque, el apricot
albóndigas, las meatballs
alcachofa, la artichoke
alérgico/a allergic
¿algo más? anything else?
algodón, el cotton
alimentación, la grocer's shop
allí there
almeja, la clam
almendra, la almond
almohada, la pillow
alpinismo, el climbing
alquilar to hire
alubias blancas, las butter beans
alubias pintas, las red kidney beans
alubias, las beans
amarillo/a yellow

ambiente, el environment
ambulancia, la ambulance
ambulatorio, el doctor's surgery
anchoa, la anchovy
andén, el platform
anfiteatro, el circle (in theatre)
angulas, las baby eels
anillo, el ring
anís, el anis
anteayer the day before yesterday
antibióticos, los antibiotics
antihistamínico, el antihistamine
aparcar to park
apartamento, el apartment, flat
aparte separate
aperitivo, el aperitif
apio, el celery
aplicar to apply
aplíquese put on/apply
aprétar to press
aquél that one
aquí here
aquí tiene here you are
arenque, el herring
arroz blanco, el boiled rice
arroz con leche, el rice pudding
arroz, el rice
asado con espetón on the spit
asado/a roast
ascensor, el lift
aseos, los toilets/cloakroom
asma, el asthma
aspirina, la aspirin
atún, el tuna
autoservicio self-service
autobús, el bus
autocar, el coach
autopista, la motorway
autovía, la A-road
avellana, la hazelnut
avería, la breakdown
aves, las poultry
ayer yesterday
ayuntamiento, el town hall
azúcar, el sugar
azul blue
azulejo, el tile

bacalao, el cod(fish)
bailar to dance

bañador, el swimming trunks
banco, el bank
baño, el bathroom
barato cheap
barca, la boat
barquillo, el ice-cream wafer
barra de pan, la loaf of bread
barrio, el town district
bastante lejos a fairly long way away
batería, la battery
batido, el milk shake
beber to drink
bebida, la drink
berenjena, la aubergine
berza, la cabbage
besugo, el sea bream
bicicleta, la bike
bien hecho/a well done (steak)
billete de ida y vuelta return ticket
billete de ida, el single ticket
billete, el ticket
bistec, el grilled steak
bizcocho, el sponge biscuit
blanco/a white
blusa, la blouse
boca, la mouth
bocadillo, el sandwich
bodega, la traditional bar
bollo, el pastry
bolsa, la bag
bolso, el handbag
bonito, el tuna
boquerón, el anchovy
bota, la boot
botella, la bottle
botón, el button
braga, la knickers
brasa, la barbecue
brazo, el arm
brocheta, la skewer, kebab
brócoli, el broccoli
buenas noches good night
buenas tardes good afternoon/evening
bueno/a good
buenos días good morning
bufanda, la scarf
buñuelo, el doughnut

caballa, la mackerel

caballeros, los gentlemen
cabeza, la head
cabina, la telephone kiosk
cabrito, el kid (baby goat)
cacahuetes, los peanuts
cacerola, la casserole
cadera, la hip
café con hielo, el iced coffee
café con leche, el creamy white coffee
café cortado, el slightly white coffee
café descafeinado, el decaffeinated coffee
café irlandés Irish coffee
café solo, el black coffee
café, el coffee
caja de tiritas, la box of sticking plaster
caja fuerte, la safe
calabacín, el courgette
calabaza, la marrow
calamar, el squid
calcetines, los socks
caldo, el clear soup
caliente hot
calle, la street
callos, los tripe
calzoncillo, el underpants
cama de niño, la child's bed
cama individual, la single bed
cama de matrimonio, la double bed
cama, la bed
camarero/a waiter/waitress
camarones, los baby prawns/shrimps
cambiar to change (money)
camisa, la shirt
camiseta, la vest/T-shirt
camping, el campsite
campo de golf, el golf course
caña, la draught beer
canelones, los cannelloni
cangrejo, el crab
caracoles de mar, los whelks
caracoles de tierra, los snails
caravana, la caravan
carnaval, el carnival
carne de vaca, la beef
carne, la meat

carnicería, la butcher's (shop)
carrete, el roll (of film)
carretera, la (main) road
cartera, la wallet
casa de huéspedes, la bed and breakfast
casco viejo old town
cassette, la cassette
castaña ,la chestnut
castillo, el castle
catedral, la cathedral
cava, el sparkling wine
caza, la game (food)
cazuela, la stew
cebolla, la onion
cena, la dinner
cenicero, el ashtray
centro (ciudad), el (town) centre
cerámica, la ceramics
cercanías, las outskirts/suburbs
cercano/a near
cerdo, el pig
cereza, la cherry
cerrado closed
cerrar to close
cervecería, la bar/pub
cerveza, la bottled beer
champán, el champagne
champiñones, los mushrooms
chaqueta, la jacket
charcutería, la delicatessen
charlar to chat
cheque de viaje, el traveller's cheque
chile, el chilli
chirimoya, la custard apple
chocolate, el hot chocolate drink/chocolate
chorizo, el spicy sausage
chucho, el sweet bun
chuleta, la chop, cutlet
churros, los fritters
cigarrillo, el cigarette
cine, el cinema
cinturón, el belt
ciruela, la plum
clara, la shandy
claro of course
coche, el car
coche de alquiler, el hire car

cocido al vapor steamed
cocido, el stew
cocido/a boiled/stewed
codo, el shoulder
col, la cabbage
colega, el/la colleague
coliflor, la cauliflower
collar, el necklace
comercio, el store
comestibles, los groceries
comisaría, la police station
comisión, la commission charge
¿cómo? pardon?
completo/a full
comprar to buy
compresas, los sanitary towels
con guía guided tour
coñac, el brandy
concierto, el concert
condón, el condom
constipado/a to have a cold
copa, la wine glass
copita, la sherry glass
corbata, la tie
cornete, el ice-cream cornet
correos post office
corrida de toros, la bullfight
cortado/a cut
creer to think/believe
crema, la cream/custard
creo I think/believe
croqueta, la croquette
cruce, el cross
crudo/a raw
cruzar to cross
cuajada, la junket
¿cuánto? how much?
¿cuánto son? how much are they?
¿cuánto tarda? how long does it take?
cubo de la basura, el dustbin
cubalibre, el white rum and coke
cubierto, el cover charge
cuello, el neck
cuenta, la bill
cuero, el leather
cuerpo, el body
¡cuidado! watch out!

dar to give

de of/from
de nada don't mention it
decir to say
dedo, el finger
¡déjeme en paz! leave me alone!
dentista, el dentist
derecha, la right hand side
desayuno, el breakfast
descansar to rest
descanso, el interval
despacio slowly
día, el day
diabético/a diabetic
diarrea, la diarrhoea
dinero, el money
discoteca, la disco
docena, la dozen
doler to hurt
dolor de cabeza, el headache
¿dónde? where?
¿dónde están? where are they?
dormir to sleep
ducha, la shower
duele it hurts
dulce sweet

embutido, el sausage
empanadilla (de carne/pescado), la small (meat/fish) pasty
empanado/a breaded and fried
empastar to fill (a tooth)
en escabeche marinated
en estado pregnant
enseguida right away
en total all together
encantado/a nice to meet you
endivias, las chicory
enfermero/a nurse
ensalada mixta, la mixed salad
ensalada, la salad
ensaladilla rusa, la Russian salad
¿entiende? do you understand?
entonces then
entrada, la ticket/entrance
entradas, las starters
entrecot, el steak
entremeses, los hors d'oeuvres
error, el mistake
escabechado/a pickled
escalera, la staircase
escarola, la endive

escribir to write
ese/a that
esos/as those
espaguetis, los spaghetti
espalda, la back
español/a Spanish
espárragos, los asparagus
espectáculo, el show
espinacas, las spinach
esposa, la wife
espumoso sparkling
esquí, el ski
esquí acuático, el water ski
esquíar to ski
esquina, la corner
estación de autobuses, la bus station
estación del ferrocarril, la railway station
estación, la station
estadio, el stadium
estanco, el tobacconist
estar to be
éste this one
estofado stewed
estreñido/a to be constipated
estudiar to study
estudio I study
excursiones, las walking
exposición, la exhibition
extranjero abroad

fabada, la white bean stew
faisán, el pheasant
falda, la skirt
farmacia de guardia, la emergency chemist
farmacia, la chemist
feria, la festival
ferretería, la hardware
ferrocarril, el railway
fiambres, los cold meats
ficha, la form
fideos, los noodles
fiebre, la fever
fiesta, la party
filete, el fillet
fin de semana, el weekend
final, el end
fino, el dry sherry
firmar to sign

flan, el creme caramel
frambuesa, la raspberry
fresa, la strawberry
fresco/a fresh
frio/a cold
frito/a fried
frutería, la fruiterer's shop
fuegos artificiales, los fireworks
fumador/no fumador smoking/non smoking
funcionar to work/function
fútbol, el football

galería de arte, la art gallery
gallina, la hen
gamba, la prawn
ganso, el goose
garbanzos, los chickpeas
garganta, la throat
garrafa, la carafe
gaseosa, la lemonade
gasolina sin plomo, la unleaded petrol
gasolina, la petrol
ginebra, la gin
gintonic, el gin and tonic
gracias thank you
grande big
granizado, el iced drink
gratuito/a free
grave serious
grifo, el tap
guantes, los gloves
guardarropa, el cloakroom
guía, la guide book
guía, el/la guide (person)
guisantes, los peas
gusto taste/choice

habas, las broad beans
habichuelas, las haricot beans
habitación doble, la double room
habitación individual, la single room
habitación, la room
hablar to speak
hablo I speak
hay there is
heladería, la ice-cream shop
helados, los ice-cream
hervido/a boiled

hielo, el ice
hierbas, las herbs
hígado, el liver
higo, el fig
hijo/a son/daughter
hinojo, el fennel
¡hola! hello!
hora, la hour
horario, el timetable
horchata, la milky, nut-based drink
hostal, el small hotel
hotel, el hotel
hoy today
hueso, el bone
huevas, las fish eggs/roe
huevos cocidos/duros, los hard boiled eggs
huevos escalfados, los poached eggs
huevos pasados por agua, los boiled eggs
huevos revueltos, los scrambled eggs
huevos, los eggs

iglesia, la church
ilimitado unlimited
incluido included
información, la information
infusión, la herbal tea
inglés/a English
interesante interesting
invierno, el winter
izquierda, la left hand side

jabalí, el wild boar
jamón de York, el boiled ham
jamón serrano, el cured ham
jamón, el ham
jarabe, el cough mixture
jarra, la pitcher
jerez, el sherry
jersey, el jumper
joyería, la jeweller's
judías blancas, las haricot beans
judías verdes, las green/French beans
judías, las beans
juguete, el toy

kilometraje ilimitado unlimited mileage

la tomamos we'll take it
laberinto, el maze
lana, la wool
langosta, la lobster
langostino, el king prawn
lavabo, el toilet
lavandería, la laundry
laxante, el laxative
le va bien it suits you
leche, la milk
lechuga, la lettuce
lejos a long way away
lengua, la tongue
lenguado, el sole (fish)
lentejas, las lentils
lentes de contacto, las contact lenses
levantarse to get up
libra, la pound (£)
libre free
libro de reclamaciones, el complaint book (in hotel)
libro, el book
liebre, la hare
limón, el lemon
limonada, la fizzy lemon drink
línea, la line
listo/a ready
llave, la key
llegar to arrive
llénelo de fill up with
llevar to wear
lo siento I'm sorry
lombarda, la red cabbage
lomo de cerdo el pork loin (pieces)
longaniza, la spicy sausage
luces (del coche), las (car) lights
luego later

magdalena, la bun
magnífico/a magnificent
mahonesa, la mayonnaise
maíz, el sweetcorn
maleta, la suitcase
maletín, el briefcase
mañana tomorrow/morning
mano, la hand

manta, la blanket
mantel, el tablecloth
mantequilla, la butter
manzana, la apple
manzanilla, la camomile tea
mapa, el map
marido, el husband
mariscada, la mixed shellfish
mariscos, los seafood
marisquería, la seafood restaurant
marrón brown
más more
más o menos more or less/about
matrícula del coche, la car registration number
mazapán, el marzipan
me gusta/n I like it/them
me llamo my name is
me lo/la llevo I'll take it
¿me puede ayudar? can you help me?
media hora, la half an hour
media pensión, la half board
medianoche, la midnight
medias, las stockings/tights
médico/a doctor
mediodía, el midday
mejillones, los mussels
melocotón, el peach
melón, el melon
membrillo, el quince/quince jelly
menú del día set lunch/dinner
mercado, el market
merienda, la afternoon snack
merluza, la hake
mermelada de naranja, la marmalade
mermelada, la jam
mes, el month
mesón, el inn/pub
metálico, el cash
miel, la honey
mirador, el viewpoint
mismo/a the same
mitad de precio half price
mixto/a mixed
moda, la fashion
moderno/a modern
monedero, el purse
monumento, el monument

monumentos, los sights
moras, las blackberries
morcilla, la black pudding
mostaza, la mustard
moto, la motorbike
motor, el engine
mover to move
muchas gracias thank you very much
mucho/a much
muchos/as many
muela, la tooth
muralla, la walls of a town
museo, el museum
música, la music
muslo, el thigh

nabo, el turnip
nada nothing
naranja orange (colour)
naranjada, las fizzy orange drink
nariz, la nose
naranja, la orange
nata, la cream
natillas, las egg custard
natural fresh/raw
negocio, el business
negro/a black
niño/a child
no no
no entiendo I don't understand
no hay we don't have any
no sé I don't know
no se preocupe don't worry
noche, la night
nombre, el name
nueces, las nuts
nuez, la nut
número, el number

ocupado/a taken/occupied
oficina de turismo, la tourist office
oído, el ear
¡oiga! excuse me/hello there!
ojos, los eyes
ópera, la opera
operar to operate
oreja, la outer ear
ostras, las oysters
otoño, el autumn
paella, la rice dish

pagar to pay
país, el country
palacio, el palace
palillo de dientes, el toothpick
palo de golf, el golf club
pan, el bread
pan tostado, el toast
pañal, el nappy
panceta, la bacon
paños higiénicos, los sanitary towels
pantalón, el trousers
papel higiénico, el toilet paper
papelería, la stationer's shop
paquete, el packet
para for
parada de taxis, la taxi rank
parada, la stop (train/bus etc)
parador, el state-run hotel
paraíso, el 'gods' (in theatre)
parque, el park
parrillada, la mixed grill
partido de fútbol, el football match
pasa, la raisin
pasado mañana the day after tomorrow
pasaporte, el passport
pasear to stroll
pastel, el cake
pastelería, la cake shop
pastilla, la pill
patata, la potato
patatas fritas, las crisps, chips
pato, el duck
pavo, el turkey
peaje, el toll
pecho, el chest
película en blanco y negro black and white film
película en color, la colour film
película, la film (for camera)
pelota, la ball
pendientes, los earrings
pensión, la boarding house
pensión completa, la full board
pepinillo, el gherkin
pepino, el cucumber
pequeño/a small
pera, la pear
perder to lose

perdido/a lost
perdiz, la the partridge
perdone excuse me
perejil, el parsley
periódicos extranjeros, los foreign newspapers
permiso de conducir, el driving licence
pero but
persiana, la blind
persona/as, la/s person/people
pescadilla, la whiting
pescaditos, los sprats
pescado, el fish
pescar to fish
pez espada, el swordfish
picadillo, el minced meat/sausage
picadura, la (insect) bite/sting
picante spicy
picatostes, los croutons
piel, la leather
pierna, la leg
pies, los feet
pila, la battery
pimiento, el pepper
pimentón (picante), el (chilli) pepper
piña, la pineapple
pinchazo, el flat tyre
pincho moruno, el marinated pork kebab
piñones, los pine kernels
pintura, la painting
piscina, la swimming pool
piso, el floor
pista de tenis, la tennis course
plancha, la iron
plancha, la windsurf board
plano, el plan
planta baja, la ground floor
planta, la floor
plátano, el banana
platea, la stalls (in theatre)
plato del día dish of the day
plato típico de aquí, el local speciality
plato, el course (of meal)
platos combinados, los set dishes
playa, la beach
plaza mayor, la main square

plaza, la square
poco little
poco hecho/a rare/underdone (steak)
poder can, be able to
poleo, el mint tea
policía, la police
poliéster, el polyester
pollo, el chicken
pomelo, el grapefruit
póngame I'll have
pónganos we'll have
por aquí this way
por favor please
postal, la postcard
postre, el sweet/dessert
preocuparse to worry
presentar to present
primavera, la spring
primero/a first
programa, el theatre programme
propina, la tip
próxima parada next stop
¿puedo probármelo/la? can I try it on?
puente, el bridge
puerro, el leek
puerto, el port
pulgar, el thumb
pulpo, el octopus
pulsera, la bracelet
puré de patatas, el mashed potatoes
puro, el cigar

¿qué desea? what would you like?
¿qué hora es? what time is it?
¿qué le pasa? what's the matter?
¿qué talla? what size?
¿qué tipo? what type?
quedar to stay
quemaduras del sol, las sun burn
querer to want
queso fresco, el curd cheese
queso, el cheese
quiere could you?
quiero I want/I'd like
quiosco de prensa, el kiosk

rábano, el radish
rabo de buey, el oxtail

ración, la portion
raciones, las bigger version of tapas
rape, el angler fish
rápido fast/quick
raqueta, la racket
raya, la sakte (fish)
rebozado/a battered, breaded and fried
receta, la prescription
recibo, el receipt
recomendar to recommend
refresco, el cold drink
rehogado/a sautéed
rellenar to fill in
relleno stuffed
reloj, el watch
relojería, la watchmaker's
remolacha, la beetroot
repetir to repeat
repollo, el cabbage
repostería, la pastries
requesón, el cream cheese
reserva, la reservation
restaurante, el restaurant
revelar to develop (film)
revista, la magazine
revuelto, el egg dish
Reyes Magos three wise men
rico/a delicious
riñón, el kidney
río, el river
rodaballo, el turbot
rodilla, la knee
rojo/a red
ron, el rum
rosbif, el roast beef
roto/a broken

saber to know
sabor, el flavour
sacar to take out (tooth)
sal, la salt
sala de baile, la dance hall
salchichón, el sausage
sale leaves
salida, la exit
salir to leave
salmón, el salmon
salmonete, el red mullet
salteado/a sautéed

salvia, la sage
sandía, la water melon
sandwich mixto, el toasted sandwich with cheese and ham
sangría, la red wine and fruit juice
sardina, la sardine
¿se necesitan? do you need?
¿se puede? can you?
sección, la department
seco/a dry
segundo/a second
seguro, el insurance
sello, el stamp
Semana Santa, la holy week
semana, la week
sencillo single
señor/a sir/madam
sepia, la cuttlefish
servicio, el toilet
servilleta, la napkin
servir to serve/help
seso, el brain
seta, la wild mushroom
sí yes
sidra, la cider
siesta, la afternoon nap
silla, la chair
sin without
sitio, el space/room
¡socorro! help!
solomillo, el sirloin steak
solución, la solution
sombrero, el hat
sombrilla, la sun shade
sopa, la soup
sorbete, el sorbet
sortija, la ring
sótano, el basement
soy I am
su his/her/its/their/your
subtítulos, los sub-titles
suéter/jersey, el jumper
supermercado, el supermarket

taberna, la bar
TALGO high-speed train
tallarines, los tagliatelle
tapas, las bar snacks
taquilla, la ticket office
tarde, la afternoon/evening
tarjeta, la card/postcard

tarjeta de crédito, la credit card
tarjeta de metro, la
metro/underground card
tarjeta telefónica, la phone card
tarta, la tart, pie
tasca, la bar
taza, la cup
té, el tea
teatro, el theatre
teleférico, el cable car
teléfono, el telephone
televisión, la television
tenemos we have
tener to have
tenga here you are
tengo I have
tercero/a third
ternera, la veal
terraza, la balcony
tiempo, el time
tienda, la shop
tienda (de campaña), la tent
tinta, la ink
tipo de cambio, el exchange rate
toalla, la towel
tobillo, el ankle
¿todo bien? everything OK?
todo recto straight on
todo/a all
tomate, el tomato
tónica, la tonic water
toro, el bull
toros los bullfighting
tortilla española, la Spanish
omelette
tos, la cough
trabajar to work
tren, el train
trucha, la trout
tu you
turrón, el nougat

urgente urgent
usted you
uvas, las grapes

vacaciones, las holiday
vainilla, la vanilla
vaqueros, los jeans
variados/as assorted
vaso, el glass

vegetariano/a vegetarian
vela, la sail
venado, el venison
vendimia, la grape harvest
ver to see
verano, el summer
¿verdad? is that right?
verde green
verdulería, la greengrocer's
verduras, las vegetables
vermut vermouth
vestido, el dress
vestuarios, los changing rooms
viaje, el trip/journey
vieira, la scallop
vinagre, el vinegar
vino blanco, el white wine
vino rosado, el rosé wine
vino tinto, el red wine
vino, el wine
vivo I live
vomitar to vomit

ya veremos we'll see
yo también so am I
yogur, el yoghurt

zanahoria, la carrot
zapatería, la shoe shop
zapato, el shoe
zumo, el juice

Titles available

For a complete languages catalogue please contact:
BBC Books, Book Service By Post,
PO Box 29,
Douglas,
Isle of Man, IM99 1BQ,
tel: 01624-675137, fax: 01624-70923

BBC books are available at all good bookshops or direct
from the publishers as above.